Montage Memories

creating altered scrapbook pages

by Erikia Ghumm & Pamela Frye Hauer

Dallas Studio
TULIA, TEXAS

MEMORY MAKERS BOOKS

Executive Editor **Kerry Arquette**   Founder **Michele Gerbrandt**

Authors and Artists **Erikia Ghumm and Pamela Frye Hauer**

Art Director **Andrea Zocchi**

Designer **Nick Nyffeler**

Photographer **Ken Trujillo**

Contributing Photographer **Christina Dooley, Brenda Martinez, Jennifer Reeves, Laura Simon**

Contributing Photo Stylists and Props **Erikia Ghumm, Pamela Frye Hauer,**

Hand Model **Erikia Ghumm**

Editorial Support **Jodi Amidei, Emily Curry Hitchingham, MaryJo Regier, Dena Twinem, Janetta Wieneke**

Montage Memories: Creating Altered Scrapbook Pages

Published by Memory Makers Books, an imprint of F & W Publications, Inc.

12365 Huron Street, Suite 500, Denver, CO 80234

Phone 1-800-254-9124

First edition. Printed in Singapore.

08 07 06 05 04 5 4 3 2 1

          Library of Congress Cataloging-in-Publication Data

Ghumm, Erikia
    Montage memories : creating altered scrapbook pages / Erikia Ghumm & Pamela Frye Hauer.
        p. cm.
    Includes bibliographical references and index.
    ISBN 1-892127-32-6
      1. Photograph albums. 2. Photographs--Conversation and restoration. 3. Scrapbooks. 4.
    Altered books. I. Hauer, Pamela Frye. II. Title.

    TR465.G49 2004
    745.593--dc22

                                        2003066604

Distributed to trade and art markets by

F & W Publications, Inc.

4700 East Galbraith Road, Cincinnati, OH 45236

Phone 1-800-289-0963

Memory Makers Books is the home of *Memory Makers*, the scrapbook magazine dedicated to educating and inspiring scrapbookers.

To subscribe, or for more information, call 1-800-366-6465. Visit us on the Internet at www.memorymakersmagazine.com.

We dedicate this book to our
spouses, family and friends who
have inspired, encouraged us and
offered unconditional support in all
of our creative endeavors.
We sincerely thank you.
Much love, Erikia & Pamela

Table of Contents

16 Backgrounds

38 Photographs

60 Lettering

84 Embellishments

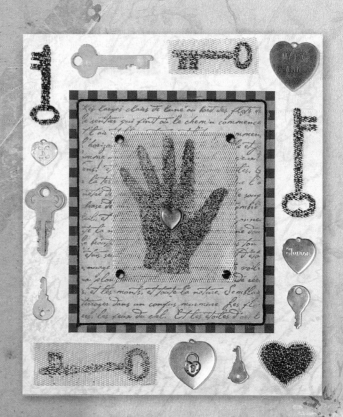

Ever since we were children, we've both been collectors of mementos, ephemera and items that some might call "junk." Being artists, we have used these collected items in our pieces over the years, sharing our finished artwork with family, friends and our communities. Our love for the collection and creation of art are just two of the many things we discovered we had in common when we met as artists for Memory Makers in 1999. The friendship that started then has continued to develop over the years although we have more recently chosen to dedicate ourselves to our work as freelance designers.

When the prospect of creating this book together was introduced by editors at Memory Makers, we were thrilled at the idea of producing a collection of work using an art style that we love and in which we have worked for many years. As we developed our ideas, we looked to art mediums outside of scrapbooking that collage and mixed-media artists have used for decades. Mixing these art forms with scrapbooking gives our layouts a unique altered look. The beauty of this type of art, in which there are really no rules to follow, results in a free-form style. Layouts can be simply designed and embellished or they can be "over the top." It all depends on your personal likes or dislikes. Because of its "loose" approach, the altered style does not need to involve enormous amounts of time, making it an option for busy scrapbook artists.

So, whether you're a beginner to altered scrapbook art or an advanced artist, we hope that you will find techniques throughout this book that will get you thinking outside of the box and that you find inspiration to experiment, create and discover this extraordinary art form!

Erikia Ghumm and Pamela Frye Hauer
Authors and Artists
Montage Memories: Creating Altered Scrapbook Pages

Tools

Pictured here are many of the basic tools needed to create "altered" art. Most of them are traditional craft and scrapbooking tools which are available at your local craft or scrapbooking store in a variety of styles and patterns. There are many things you can find around the house that also make terrific tools for creating altered art. You'll find them in your bathroom, office, garage and even your kitchen. An old spoon can become a handy burnishing tool, for example. Like the art itself, the tools used to create it are only limited by your imagination!

Tools

Mini stapler

Scissors

Craft knife

Piercing tool

Wood stylus

Bone folder

Wire brush

Needle-nose pliers

Eyelet setter

Hole punch

Needles

Brayer

Sandpaper

Colorants

Colored pencils

Paint pen

Ink

Acrylic paint

Fine-point pen

Photo-tinting pen

Dual-tipped marker

Adhesives

Tab applicator

Tape runner

Silicone adhesive

Wet adhesive

Glue dots

Stamping Colorants

Pigment rainbow ink pad

Metallic rub-ons

Black felt ink pad

Colored dye ink pad

Embossing powder

Embossing embellishments

Pigment powder

Small Hammer
Metal Ruler

Stamping

Block pattern stamp

Design stamp

Object stamp

Label stamp

Roller stamp

Chemicals

Stamp pad cleaner

Adhesive remover

De-acidification spray

UV inhibitor

Applicators

Dusting brush

Stylus tip stamp

Paintbrushes

Sea sponge

Brush sponge

Comb

Ink pen

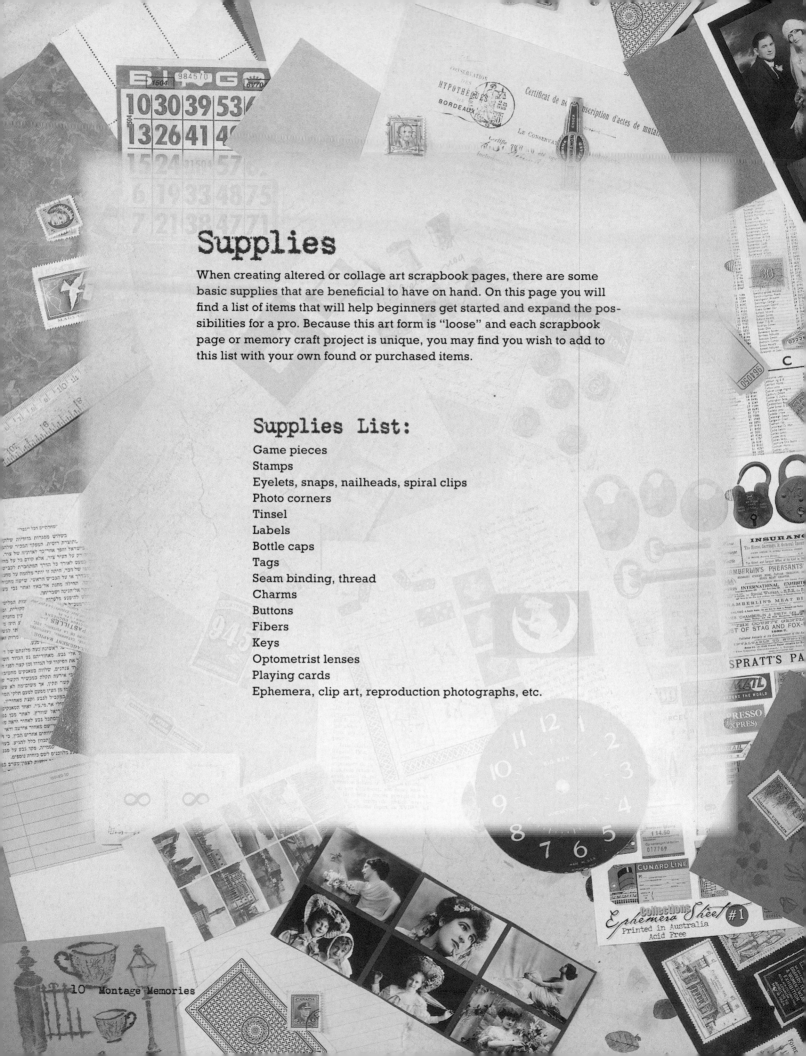

Supplies

When creating altered or collage art scrapbook pages, there are some basic supplies that are beneficial to have on hand. On this page you will find a list of items that will help beginners get started and expand the possibilities for a pro. Because this art form is "loose" and each scrapbook page or memory craft project is unique, you may find you wish to add to this list with your own found or purchased items.

Supplies List:

Game pieces
Stamps
Eyelets, snaps, nailheads, spiral clips
Photo corners
Tinsel
Labels
Bottle caps
Tags
Seam binding, thread
Charms
Buttons
Fibers
Keys
Optometrist lenses
Playing cards
Ephemera, clip art, reproduction photographs, etc.

Customizing Pre-made Albums

As scrapbooking has grown in popularity over the last decade, manufacturers of the craft's tools and supplies have stretched themselves to meet artists' needs. They have introduced products that cover the spectrum in design and color and albums that make it possible for scrapbookers to work in smaller and larger formats. Many of these albums can be customized to reflect the personality of the artist, the theme of the pages and the altered art style.

Tag Book Album

Add journaling and photos to make an album out of a tiny tag book.

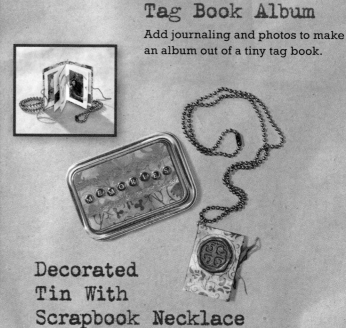

Erikia's Scrapbook 12 x 12" Post-Bound Album

Decorating an album cover does not have to be complex. A simply decorated tag that features a stamped background, a title made from letter stickers and plastic office label maker is completed with stamping ink wiped on its edges. Attach the tag to the cover with contrasting ribbon.

Decorated Tin With Scrapbook Necklace

Enclose an embellished mini scrapbook necklace inside an empty stamping ink pad tin that is adorned with torn printed papers, glitter and brads with rub-on letters.

Memories 12 x 12" Post-Bound Album

Adorn a 12 x 12" post-bound red gingham album that holds cherished memories with vintage silk fabric and 3-D typewriter keys.

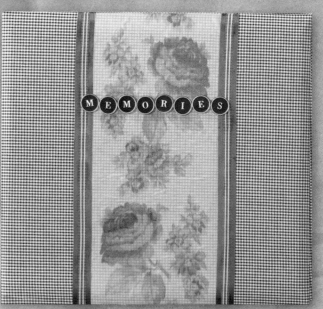

B&W 10x10" Spiral-Bound Album

A vintage frame that holds an artsy black-and-white photograph of a camera sets the theme for this 10 x 10" spiral-bound album. It is further adorned with vintage and handmade game letters, typewriter keys with metal rims set with dimensional glue, and ribbons.

Safety and Archival Issues

Altered scrapbook pages are intended to look charmingly aged and worn. In order to achieve the "look," scrapbookers may have to compromise on archival safety issues. Published books most often do not contain paper that is acid- or lignin-free and supplies and photos placed in these books may deteriorate over time. Some of the products used to accomplish the techniques featured in this book may also harm photos and memorabilia. For this reason it is vitally important that you use copies of photos and memorabilia when working on altered pages. Here are more safety tips to keep in mind.

Spray old paper ephemera with a de-acidifying spray

Use acid-free papers, inks and adhesives when possible

Buffer your photos by inserting archival paper between them and materials that may harm them

Use color copies of old items such as newspaper clippings and letters instead of the originals

Seal yellowing ephemera with acid-free laminating sheets

Use matte paper rather than glossy paper when printing photos on your home printer

Accordion Album

Create a mixed-media 3-D assemblage which pays tribute to family members inside the cut-out window of an accordion album. It is embellished with a rusted heart, watch face, letter and glass beads, wire, locket frame and a cyanotype photograph.

Dream, Art, Create 11x14" Hidden Spiral-Bound Album

Several types of purchased and handmade metal words describe the contents of this creative 11 x 14" hidden spiral-bound scrapbook that is framed by acrylic paint and glitter glue.

Album Bindings and Alternative Photo Containment Options

If a pre-made album isn't right for your altered project, try binding an album of your own or turning a 3-D item into a cool memory craft. There are no rules when it comes to creativity, which opens up a plethora of possibilities for storing your photos and memorabilia. Here are a few great ideas for creative containment.

Tobacco Tin with Accordion-Fold Pages

A vintage tobacco tin turns into an artsy scrapbook when decorated with stamped papers, collaged ephemera, a button and ribbon. Inside the tin resides accordion-folded pages made from cardstock.

Hand-Bound Album

Hand bind a vintage paint-by-numbers album using loose-leaf paper rings, decorative eyelets, ribbon and a title made from 3-D typewriter keys on a printed paper mat.

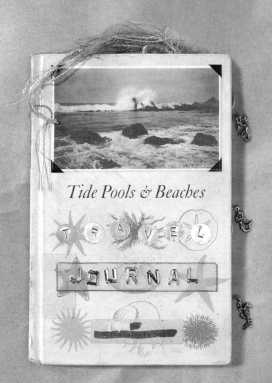

Hand-Bound Tag Album

Tags make hand binding an album easy. Add strength to the cover with laminate and copper tape. Decorate it with a cut opening framed with a slide mount that reveals a butterfly transparency layered over a vintage book page.

Altered Book

A discarded book from a school library becomes a prized travel scrapbook when it is adorned with a digital reproduction of a vintage postcard. The postcard is tinted using stamping inks. The word "travel" is stamped and punched out of metal foil, and the word "journal" is comprised of nailhead letters atop vellum.

Dog Shadow Box

Create your piece in a shadow box, so it can be hung on the wall and enjoyed every day.

Travel Journal

Use a binding punch and discs to create a custom travel journal.

8 Ball Box

Transform a round cardboard box with rubber stamps, embossing powder and vintage embellishments.

Little Fashion Book

Purchase an album kit that includes a cover ready for a photo and pages waiting to be decorated and bound with fibers or raffia.

Where to Find "Treasures" for Your Altered Scrapbook Projects

If you don't own a collection of old books, photographs, greeting cards, game pieces, vintage buttons, ticket stubs and other "treasures" go on a hunt to find them:

Ask your relatives and friends if they have vintage treasures in their garages or attics

Shop hobby stores for product lines that offer reproductions of vintage images and objects

Find second-hand ephemera and photos at thrift stores, antique stores, yard and estate sales

Shop Web site stores and online auction sites

Study newspaper classifieds

Browse flea markets and swap meets

Recycle magazines, catalogs, cards, food labels and gift wrap

Search through your junk drawers for fun paper napkins, restaurant matchbook covers, postcards and tourist brochures

Look down to find interesting, weathered items on the ground on sidewalks, playgrounds and alleys

Pets Album

Roughly stack and fold 8½ x 11" sheets of paper in half, punch two holes and weave through them with colorful ribbon.

Chapter #One
Backgrounds

Creating handmade backgrounds for scrapbook pages gives them an artistic quality that is truly distinctive. If you stretch your imagination and open your eyes wide, you'll find numerous ways to create artistic backgrounds that call on craft techniques outside the average scrapbooking realm. Creating your own backgrounds for scrapbook pages allows you to customize the look, assuring it will work strongly to support your page theme, color and photographs. In this chapter you'll discover techniques for:

Coloring backgrounds in altered books and on scrapbook pages using stamping inks, craft inks and acrylic paints

Creating traditional and digital collages using ephemera, magazine images and other types of paper materials

Recycling scrap papers for use in handmade papers and mosaics

Making custom clip art backgrounds

Using laminate to encapsulate various materials

Once you explore these and other techniques featured in this chapter, you'll be on your way to creating backgrounds for altered pages that exhibit texture, depth, style and the illusion of graceful age.

Brayer Painting

Reminiscent of well-worn antiques or weathered wood, brayer painting brings warmth and texture to scrapbook pages through a simple technique. The subtle distressed look lends itself well to scrapbook pages because it can be easily applied to a variety of surfaces, tying all of the elements together. Almost any material can be enhanced with this technique including cardstock and printed paper backgrounds, vellum, fabric and wood. Try also distressing other elements such as die cuts and stickers to embellish a brayer-painted background.

Supplies Needed: Craft ink, brayer, palette, newsprint

Erikia Ghumm
Photo Brian Ghumm

Mother Sweet As a Rosé

A dense black foam roller and black, terra cotta and orange craft ink were all it took to pull the elements of this spread together. The background, torn paper strips, tag and balsa wood strips used for the title were brayer painted at the same time and then mounted. While this page calls on subdued color combinations, you can achieve an equally, although different, effect using more exuberant colors.

"Experiment with different colorant mediums like inks, paints and dyes on a wide range of materials for very different effects."

A vintage tablecloth takes on a well-used look when painted with sepia colored craft ink.

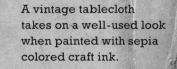

Feminine printed paper turns shabby chic with a light coat of burnt sienna and yellow ocher paint applied with a dense black foam roller. .

Soar

Use up leftover paint on smaller projects such as this card. The piece was created using acrylic paints brayered onto a piece of inkjet transparency. The butterfly stamp image was made using a black solvent-based ink pad.

Velvet paper is faux mottled to appear suede-like when painted with yellow, red and green acrylic paints which were applied with a hard rubber roller.

"For a cheap paint palette use a paper plate or a water resistant material such as a folded square of aluminum."

Delicate handmade paper is given depth when brayer-painted with rust and raisin colored stamping dye inks that are applied with a hard rubber roller.

1 Gather all of the materials to be painted. Spread the work surface with a large sheet of waxed paper. Place a dense black foam roller into the brayer. Pour several colors of craft ink onto a palette and run the brayer through the ink to slightly mix it and coat the roller. With a light touch, roll the brayer across the cardstock. Overlap strokes to cover the entire surface. Allow to dry completely.

Masking Words and Images

Utilize the text on the page of a book to create poignant journaling blocks for your scrapbook page. Mask words and images before colorizing the page and then expose them once again so their message pops. Use a variety of art materials to add customized color to the pages including ink, ink pads, acrylic paint and chalk. Just remember that the wetter your colorant, the more substantial the page must be to hold up. If you are working with thin pages, adhere several pages together beneath the page on which you are working together to form a substantial base.

Supplies Needed: Ink, sponge, waxed paper, removable artist tape, scratch paper

Erikia Ghumm

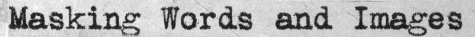

Look for a Starfish

All it takes to create this ocean-colored background is ink and a sponge. This aquatic spread, created within a book titled, *Tide, Pools and Beaches*, draws on the book's text to carry the theme. Pertinent words were masked off, the page was lightly painted and, once dried, the masked words were exposed. Photos were added, journaling and embellishments hung from eyelets on the side of the page. A stamped image completes the layout.

1 Select a book which works well with the theme of your photos. Use artist tape and scrap paper to mask off words and images that can be featured for journaling or support art on your finished scrapbook page.

2 Apply various colors of ink to the edge of a sponge. Be sure to cover the entire edge of the sponge to ensure smooth application.

3 Place a piece of waxed paper underneath the page that will be inked. Beginning in the center of the book, run the inked sponge over the page from top to bottom. Apply more ink to the sponge as needed. Ink both pages and allow them to dry before carefully removing the masks.

Scanning and Copying Images

Use pieces of ephemera and memorabilia to create custom backgrounds that allow you to keep the original items safe and intact. The simplest way to achieve these customized effects is to scan a single item, such as a letter, and print it to fill an 8½ x 11" sheet of acid-free paper. If your printer does not print to the edge of the page, simply mount or mat the printed sheet to bring it up to size. You may also wish to scan an arrangement of items and print them to create your unique background.

Supplies Needed: Home computer, scanner and printer,
vintage paper ephemera, cardstock

Pamela Frye Hauer

Create an arresting background by scanning an array of objects. Arrange pieces such as school papers, report cards and graduation announcements, keeping in mind your concept for the final layout. Work around those spots in which you plan to eventually mount photos and other elements. Once complete, add photos and embellishments such as stamps, charms or game pieces to your finished page, or wrap fiber around the edges of a playing card to add visual interest.

Scan Varied Objects
to Create Customized Backgrounds

Old photos, pictures from vintage books or magazines, and 3-D items such as keys or leaves can be scanned to create interesting papers. Cloth with neat designs or textures and vintage clothing can make fun images as well. Enlarge a detail to fill the page like the postage stamp shown. Create great patterns and textures by enlarging printed items so the "half-tone" dots used to print are visible or even greatly exaggerated.

"Customize your scanned images by adjusting the scanner's settings or utilizing the versatility of your photo imaging software. If the image you have scanned is too dark or strong, print it at less than 100 percent opacity for a softer look. Change the tone or the entire color of the image so it will coordinate with other page elements."

"For a different look and feel, scan and print pieces of ephemera individually. Cut out each printed item. Use the pieces to create a collage. If you wish, you may scan the completed collage and use that as your background page."

Inking Embossed Paper

Accentuating embossed papers with an ink pad brings out their beauty. Like a valued antique, embossed papers that are colored with an ink pad have a distinguished antique patina, adding interest and texture without bulk. Most textured paper surfaces can be easily transformed. Try experimenting with pre-embossed papers or make your own textured papers by folding, crumpling, crimping or dry embossing ordinary cardstock.

Supplies Needed: Purchased and hand embossed papers, ink pad with removable lid

Erikia Ghumm

The Cunning Cat

Reach for a variety of pre-embossed and hand embossed papers to create this purr-fect page. The inked embossed background paper was made prior to assembling the page. A letter template helped create the page title, which was dry embossed on cardstock using a stylist. The journaling words "Baby 10 years old January 2002" were cut from cream cardstock and run through an office label maker (the type that uses a roll of plastic sticker strips). A crimped photo mat provides a platform for "Cat."

Memories of Grandma Ann Box and Tuck-away Album

A satin mache` book box and a hand-bound album take on an elegantly aged look reminiscent of years gone by. Decoupage the box with crumpled gold paper, thick corrugated paper, and an embossed rose sticker that have been colorized with sepia colored inks.

"For best results use dye ink when coloring lighter papers and pigment ink when coloring darker papers."

1 To ink over embossed or textured papers, remove the lid from the ink pad. (Some hinged lids are made to be snapped off.) Lay the ink pad directly on the paper you wish to colorize. Run it over the surface in a light, circular motion until the desired effect is achieved. Multiple colors can be used; however, begin with the lightest color first.

Laminating Layers

Paper, stickers, confetti, photos and other flat objects can be sandwiched between laminating sheets to create your own personalized mini album. Laminating sheets, available in matte or gloss finishes and in several sizes, sport a peel-off backing which can be removed to expose a sticky surface. By placing photos, double-sided papers and decorative materials between two sheets of the lamination you can form a sturdy page that can be viewed from both sides and safely protects photos and other elements.

Supplies Needed: Laminating sheets; photographs; paper; embellishments such as tinsel, confetti, fibers, stickers, stamps, charms and ephemera; 1/8" hole punch; needle-nose pliers; assorted jump rings; scissors and craft knife; wet and dry adhesives

Pamela Frye Hauer

Live, Love, Laugh

This neat little laminated album was made by sandwiching double-sided papers, confetti, tinsel and other paper objects such as stamped blocks between three sheets of laminate paper. Word stickers and other 3-D accents were adhered on top of the sealed page. Create additional pages in a similar fashion. When complete, punch 1/8" holes along the edge of the front cover about 1/4" from the page edge. The cover acts as a guide for punching holes in the additional pages. Use jewelry jump rings and needle-nose pliers to bind the pages together. Create the page title with charming stickers.

"Don't stop with two layers of laminate. For a more complex look, layer additional items on the outside of one of your sealed laminate pages. Secure the added items with a third sheet of laminate. Repeat until you're happy with the result."

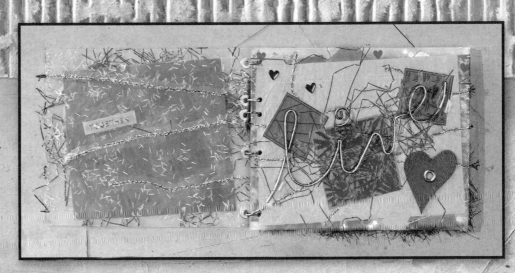

"Use laminate sheets to create mini albums to be included within larger albums. Attach them directly into the binding or adhere them to the page to hold extra photos or journaling."

"If the edges of your laminate sheets are not perfectly aligned, trim them with scissors or a craft knife. You can also trim away fibers and tinsel that extend beyond the page edges or allow them to project beyond the page edges, depending upon the desired effect."

You have a keen sense of humor and love a good time.

Live, Love, Laugh Pages

Decorate your laminated pages with dramatic wire words, jewels, velvet and charm hearts. Add mini boas, a fortune cookie prediction, brads and other elements for extra wow and whimsy.

Using Clip Art

Customize backgrounds so that they work with scrapbook pages of any theme through the use of clip art and a home printer. There are uncountable numbers of clip art designs available including abstract designs, shapes and patterns. Find great clip art in books, CD-ROMs and on the Internet, as well as on popular computer programs. You may also choose to scan illustrations or backgrounds from vintage books to use in your background designs.

Supplies Needed: Clip art, home computer and printer, colored paper

Pamela Frye Hauer

"Save money on printing mistakes by printing a 'test run' using the ink-saving mode on your computer and plain paper."

Elitch Lanes - Denver, Colorado

April 19th 2003
Ronnie & I went bowling with Lizzie & Dean. She & I were both still pregnant. When we got to our lane, a guy exclaimed "You swallowed a bowling ball." It sure looked like it! With my big stomach and a sore hip, I could barely throw the ball and Ronnie had to play the second game for me!

"When planning to use a large clip art image, take the time to fully design your layout prior to beginning work. This will ensure space for the image and the artistic balance of the final product."

I Swallowed a Bowling Ball

Use your home computer and printer to create simple designs which feature one large image per page. Print a black image on solid colored paper, or experiment with printing the image in color onto printed paper. Complete the page with tiny bowling charms, ripped and stamped borders and other embellishments. Add photos and journaling.

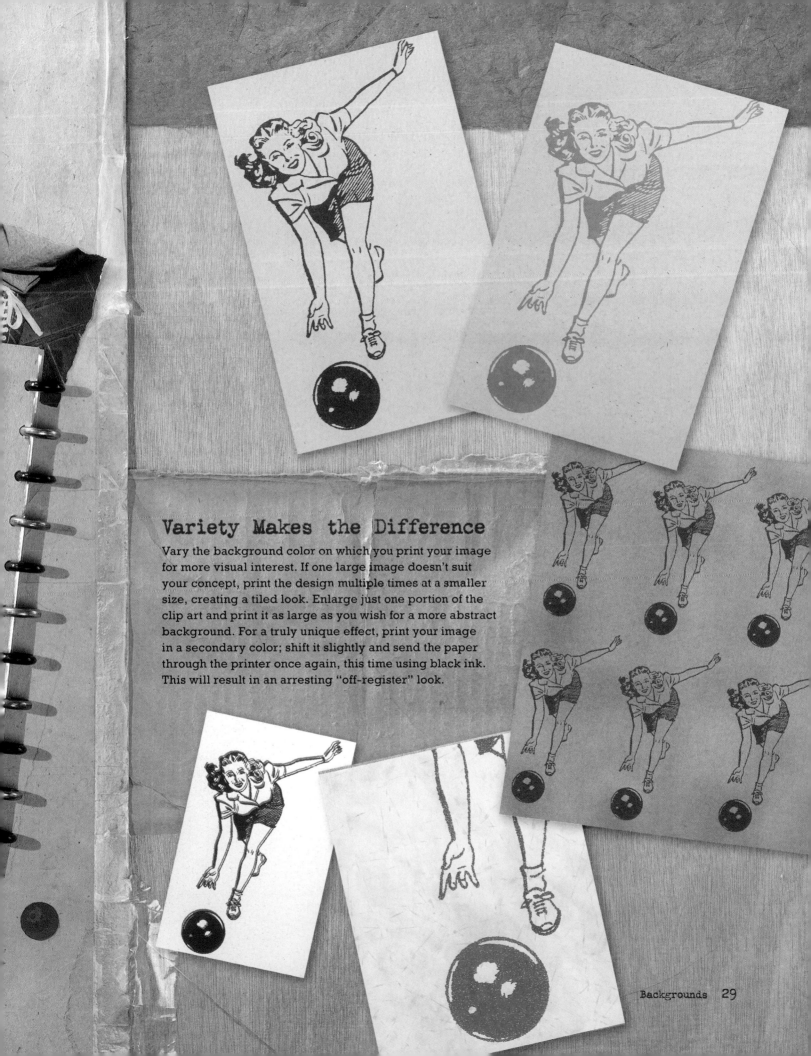

Variety Makes the Difference

Vary the background color on which you print your image for more visual interest. If one large image doesn't suit your concept, print the design multiple times at a smaller size, creating a tiled look. Enlarge just one portion of the clip art and print it as large as you wish for a more abstract background. For a truly unique effect, print your image in a secondary color; shift it slightly and send the paper through the printer once again, this time using black ink. This will result in an arresting "off-register" look.

Making Handmade Paper

Luxurious handmade paper adds an extraordinary quality to any scrapbook page. Making your own paper is a fabulous way to use up scrap paper and recycle materials such as junk mail, package labeling, dried flowers, old books and ribbon. When making paper from non-scrapbook materials, an additive can be used to make the paper acid-free. The supplies for making paper can be purchased in a kit or, if you're handy with tools, can be handmade following instructions readily available in many books.

Supplies Needed: Cardstock torn or cut into small pieces, inclusions such as dried flowers and old book pages, large tub or dishpan, blender, cookie tray, couch sheets, tools for creating your own paper-making kit, heavy books, paper press or an iron. You may also purchase a ready-made kit which may include paper molds, screens and other accessories.

Erikia Ghumm

A Surprise Bouquet

"Experiment with various types of adhesives when working with handmade paper. Strong dry adhesives such as double-sided tape and glue dots work well, as do sewing, stapling and attaching paper to the background with eyelets. Keep in mind that liquid glue may cause the pages to wave and buckle."

Make a gift of flowers last longer than a week and capture its sweet memory by adding dried petals to handmade paper. The colorful papers in this layout have inclusions of dried flowers from the bouquet, cut up pages from an old book and manufactured dried flower petals and mesh paper. To combine all of the elements and play up the handmade quality, the papers are machine stitched and adorned with ribbon and reproduction ephemera.

1 To fill an 8½ x 11" hand mold, tear an 8½ x 14" sheet of paper into small pieces. Place pieces in a blender with 2 cups of water. Blend for about 30 seconds. Pour the paper pulp into a hand mold, set in a tub of water. Use your fingers to evenly spread the pulp in the mold. Add inclusions to the surface of the pulp.

2 Lift the mold out of the tub, keeping it level. Allow the water to drain from the pulpy paper. Set the mold on a cookie sheet and remove the hand mold. Place a cover screen over the newly formed piece of paper. Begin to remove the excess water by pressing down hard with a sponge on top of the cover screen, wringing it out each time until there is no water left.

3 Remove the cover screen from the sheet of paper and place it facedown onto a couch sheet. Remove more water with the sponge pressing down hard and wringing it out each time. Remove the paper making screen carefully and place another couch sheet on top of the paper. Using a hard plastic bar press, it down hard on top of the paper removing the remaining water in the sheet of paper.

4 Carefully remove the paper from the couch sheets. To dry the paper, place it between dry couch sheets with heavy books on top or in a paper press, changing the sheets as they absorb the moisture. If the paper is needed soon after making, dry it using an iron without steam and cover with a thin cloth.

Creating a Decoupage Collage

Magazine and catalog pictures can be combined with decoupage medium to produce wonderful collage decoupage backgrounds and embellishments. Decoupage medium, a thin paste sold at art and craft stores, is available in clear or antique, matte, satin and glossy finishes. It is easy to use and easy to clean up with water. To create collage decoupage art, carefully cut around the images you've selected. Place the images facedown on scrap paper and paint a thin layer of the decoupage medium over them. Apply the images to your background page in a pleasing pattern. Once the pieces are dried, paint over the entire surface of the page with decoupage paste.

Supplies Needed: Images of flowers cut out of catalogs or magazines, antique decoupage finish, printed paper, rolling pattern stamp

Pamela Frye Hauer
Photo Lester Frye

The Foreigner

Flowers cut from magazines are decoupaged to form this wild and wonderful scrapbook page. When cutting elements to include in a collage decoupage layout, be sure to cut just inside the border lines of the image, removing all of the background from which it is cut. The natural ripple and curl that happens when images are decoupaged adds to the art's charm. This completed and dried page was stamped before the photo was mounted. Charms and a beaded necklace round out the page theme.

"Produce different looks by varying your top coat brush strokes when applying decoupage medium. Make numerous small, choppy strokes, or long curvy ones to add subtle texture to the final piece. More than one topcoat can be applied if desired, to make the decoupage finish thicker and shinier. Sprinkle fine glitter or crafting dusts onto the wet medium to add additional shine and shimmer."

Time Flies

Clippings of clocks decoupaged onto the album page were decorated with a handwriting stamp inked in silver to create this classic background. Framed images and a mesh ribbon border strip embellished with title letters, tags and letter dice create a layout with appeal that with survive the test of time.

"Before throwing away old catalogs and magazines, cut out images that appeal to you including pictures of flowers, clocks, animals, jewelry, waves, rocks and anything else that can be silhouetted. Put these pictures in a clip file, organizing the clippings in labeled envelopes so you can easily find them when working on your next project."

Making Faux Mosaics

Layouts featuring paper mosaics are not new to scrapbooking, but "grouting" the spaces between paper or photo pieces brings a different slant to the craft. The look and feel of a mosaic is strongly influenced by the types and styles of paper used to create the "tiles" and the materials used for "grout" including sand, glitter, embossing powder and finely ground mica. Experiment by mixing different mediums to create custom grout that works with your photos and the page theme.

Supplies Needed: Printed and stamped papers, square punch, sheet adhesive, black sand with glitter

Erikia Ghumm

"Make tiles out of scrap paper or recycle pages from magazines or books."

"The surfaces of mosaics are textured, making it a challenge to adhere photos, journaling blocks and embellishments to the page. For best results, use double-sided tape or adhesive dots, which have a very strong bond."

Best Friends

The artistic tiles used to create the background for this page are made from different types of printed and metallic paper which have been stamped. A mixed "grout" of sand and glitter was added between the paper tiles. Once complete, the background was embellished with dimensional epoxy stickers, a faux wax seal and journaling for a page that speaks with emotion.

1 Punch out squares from printed and stamped papers and set them aside. Apply a sheet of adhesive to a cardstock base and peel off the top protective sheet to expose the adhesive. Apply the tiles to the adhesive base leaving a small space between squares.

2 After all of the "tiles" have been applied to the adhesive base, rub their surface with a burnishing tool to make sure they are well-adhered. Working over a sheet of paper, sprinkle the mixed sand and glitter "grout" over the tiles and firmly press the grout into the crevices. Tap off the excess grout and lightly brush or wipe off any that remains.

The Eriksen Family 1970's

The face on this vintage-style photo clock is turned into a faux mosaic by using cut-out circles from printed transparency sheets for "titles" and silver leafing for the "grout". The photographs clipped around the clock's perimeter were computer manipulated and printed on photo quality paper. They are then punched into circular shapes and matted on cardstock.

Cutting Stencils

Use a custom-made stencil to decorate papers with unique, layered designs. While there are thousands of preprinted papers available, it is not always possible to find one that is just right for your artwork. This project enables you to pick the patterns and shades you like.

Supplies Needed: Pencil, craft knife, templates or patterns, cardstock, paper, ink pads, makeup sponges or other applicators

Pamela Frye Hauer
Photo Ronnie Hauer

If I could time it right
I'd be with you tonight
Out among the stars
Is that where you are?
I keep callin' to my
my Baby Blue,
my Baby Blue...
John Hiatt

"If using transparent colorants, you'll often achieve a better result by beginning with the lightest colors and moving toward darker shades with each rotation."

My Baby Blue

A beautiful stenciled background of stars and moons supports this one-of-a-kind baby page. Quirky charms, word stickers, a poetic journaling block composed of song lyrics and random metallic paper strips round out the theme. When working with this technique, simple shapes and solid background colors often work best, however softly patterned papers can also be used for beautiful effects, as can opaque metallics.

Memories

Create this album cover by cutting stencil shapes from a sheet of cardstock. Use a sponge to apply black ink through the stencil openings. Dry. Slightly shift the stencil. Use a piece of crumpled plastic to apply silver ink for a mottled, artistic effect.

"Experiment by stamping designs with rubber stamps over the stencil openings after ink has dried, for a multi-image effect."

1 Create a stencil from a sheet of cardstock which is approximately the same size as your background paper. Use templates, die cuts or simple stamps to create a random design on the cardstock. Use a sharp craft knife to cut out the shapes and discard them.

2 Choose the paper onto which you plan to transfer your design (solid colors are best, but gently patterned papers can work). Lay the stencil on top of the paper. Holding it down securely use a brush or sponge to apply baby blue stamping inks or chalks through the stencil windows.

3 After coloring the first layer in baby blue, turn the stencil slightly and apply a contrasting color of opaque ink. Turn the stencil twice more, applying colorants after each turn.

4 Your finished background paper features a stunning symmetrical design.

Chapter #Two
Photographs

When creating altered scrapbook pages, the easiest way to get "the look" is by manipulating photographs to achieve additional flair and flavor. There are many techniques that can be applied to create extraordinary images from everyday shots, and while each provides a distinct look, all will inevitably draw a viewer's eye to the photos. The techniques in this chapter will help you learn how to manipulate photographs by:

Printing them on alternative surfaces using a home computer, copier or a light-sensitive cyanotype photographic paper

Transferring them onto laminate or glass

Embellishing the images with dimensional items

Applying colorants or aging the pictures

Creating photo montages

Artistically cropping, silhouetting or tearing pictures

Manipulating photographs through these and other methods introduced in this chapter is an art that looks complicated, but is easily managed once you understand the techniques. Whether manipulating modern or vintage photos, these techniques are sure to shine the spotlight on your subject.

Transferring Photos Onto Laminate

Change the look of your pages easily by transferring color photocopies of your pictures onto acid-free scrapbooking laminate. These transfers produce images that are semi-transparent with a rough-looking finish. Laminate transfers work great on scrapbook pages or in altered books for an artistic look. When working in an altered book, the pages are not acid-free. This transfer technique allows you to add photographic images without worrying about their safety.

Supplies Needed: Color photocopies of photos, solid sheet adhesive, burnisher, shallow tub, laminate

Erikia Ghumm

Florida, a Journey

Create this beautiful page by layering pieces of torn book pages and torn and inked patterned papers across the spread of an old published book. Age adhered layers with stamping inks and rub-ons. Create laminated photo transfers and mount them into the book using sheet adhesive. Accent the design with stamped images, journaling, tag, stickers and a wire word.

1 Make a color copy of a photograph on regular copy paper. Apply laminate to the front of the copied photo. Turn over the image and burnish firmly to adhere the layers together. Trim off excess laminate and paper from the image.

2 Put the laminated photo into a small tray of warm water until the paper backing is absorbed, approximately two minutes. Carefully rub off the paper, exposing the image left behind on the laminate.

"Laminate transfers don't have to be adhered with sheet adhesive. Try attaching them to your background with eyelets, brads, staples and paper clips."

3 Gently pat the transfer dry with a paper towel. If desired, the image can be given a more altered look by scratching off the edges on the backside. Apply the transfer to sheet adhesive, trim off the excess and apply to your project.

"When transferring color or black-and-white photographic images to laminate you must work with photocopies. The ink (toner) used to make the photocopy is necessary for the transfers because other inks will run when wet."

Creating Photo Montages

Use copies of modern and heritage photographs to create whimsical montages that bring together generations separated by time and tide. Look through your old and new photographs for people and things that can be easily silhouetted. Make copies of the photos, and begin carefully cutting around the figures. Play with the placement of your silhouetted photos, moving them around on the background paper or secondary photo before adhering them in a scene that is perfect in its irony.

Supplies Needed: Heritage and contemporary photographs, scissors, craft knife, adhesive

Pamela Frye Hauer

King of the Hill

Create abstract montages by combining vintage portraits with natural and architectural elements to create surreal surroundings for your relatives. Layouts can be dramatically compelling, humorous and ultimately artistic. Embellish with multiple elements including stamps, old receipts, text torn from books, postcards, flat stones or tiny game board letters.

A Great Greeting

Boys will be boys, no matter where you find them. Create an abstract montage combining young boys with old and new scenery that proves the old adage true.

Family Reunion

Time moves on and generations turn over but that certain set of eyes, that family nose and smile can be passed on. Place yourself among those whose history is your own by joining a reunion that happened before you were born.

Grandma's Home

Welcome not only your grandmother, but her house and truck, to your neighborhood with whimsical montaging. Plant a few bright flowers and place Grandma close enough to smell their scent.

Papa's Lap

How can this young man maintain his dignity when saucily dressed young women are perched on his tabletop and rockers are balanced on his shoulder and knee? He may be more tolerant because those who join him in this montage are his own offspring.

Printing Cyanotypes

Cyanotypes, also known as shadowgraphs, blue prints and nature prints, are an alternative photographic process that does not require a darkroom. This old and very simple method of reproducing pictures can be used to re-create photographs and other flat objects. The beauty of cyanotypes is not only found in the deep Prussian blue color of the print, but also their archival nature. Just treat these prints like any other photograph and they will be enjoyed for years to come.

Supplies Needed: Pretreated cyanotype paper, stiff board, piece of glass with smooth edges or a contact printing frame, rinsing tray, rubber gloves or tongs, black-and-white negatives, paper towels

Erikia Ghumm
Photo Brian Ghumm

photo shoot on CU campus Boulder, CO. 93

"Deepen the color of prints by adding a teaspoon of hydrogen peroxide to the rinse water."

let the beauty we love be what we do. -rumi

Photo Shoot

Reproduce a photo by printing black-and-white negatives directly onto cyanotype paper resulting in an image the same size as the original negative. Use these tiny photos in frames on scrapbook pages, or on large mats for an artsy look. To reproduce larger images, get creative and make custom black-and-white negatives by scanning or copying photographs onto transparency sheets. Once the cyanotype images are printed and dried, give them an artistic look by layering them on top of a graphic-printed paper and embellish with metal accents and fibers.

The Hall Family Accordion Album

Assemble a mix of family cyanotypes in a stamped accordion album on collaged tags that feature stickers and printed papers. Age the pieces with stamping ink and journal with a calligraphy pen and ink.

1 Set up a work area with enough room for a tray of water and a surface on which you can spread materials and photos to dry. On top of a stiff board or contact printing frame layer pretreated cyanotype paper, negatives and a sheet of glass. All layers should make tight contact. Expose the layered elements to the sun for a few minutes (follow cyanotype paper package directions).

2 Remove the exposed print from the work surface and rinse it in the tub of water for about two minutes. Lightly blot with paper towels to absorb excess moisture and allow it to dry.

"Caution! Cyanotypes are made of paper treated with light-sensitive chemicals. As with any chemicals, some precautions need to be taken. Never use any of your tools used in printing for the preparation or serving of food. Do not allow the chemicals to come in contact with surfaces where food is prepared. Wear rubber gloves or use tongs to handle wet prints."

Printing on Alternative Surfaces

There are many fun alternatives to printing photos on plain white paper when using your home computer system. Photo paper is available in a variety of different finishes including matte, satin and glossy, and each produces a different finished effect. Try printing scanned or digital photos directly onto thin and lightly textured scrapbooking and art papers, fabric or other surfaces for a very different look and feel.

Supplies Needed: Home computer, scanner and printer, traditional or digital photograph, printed paper

Pamela Frye Hauer

Midnight

Print a photo on patterned paper for an upbeat look. When using printed papers, choose those that are neither too dark nor have bold patterns, as these may cause your photo to "disappear." Draw even more interest to your photo by wrapping it in fiber. Adorn the page with letter stamps, stickers, ribbon and journaling.

Printing on Specialty Papers and Other Surfaces

The surface on which a photo is printed strongly impacts the way the picture will both look and feel. Mulberry and handmade paper, "velvet" paper, canvas, brown paper bags and even shrink plastic offer unique effects for pages of all styles and themes.

"Printing on alternative surfaces works nicely with black-and-white photographs, but color photos can produce interesting effects as well. Photos can be printed on any color vellum, but must be printed with a laser, rather than inkjet, printer. Try printing on acetate that has been specifically manufactured for printing as well."

Transferring Photos Onto Glass

Transferring treasured photographs to glass gives them a look that is totally unique. Its sleek, smooth and transparent quality adds a look of weight to the delicate transferred images. There are various ways to transfer images to glass, but none is easier than using a sheet adhesive in conjunction with an image which has been printed or copied onto a transparency sheet. You can transfer an image to any smooth, flat glass surface using this technique. Try layering glass-transferred photographs on top of stamped, printed or hand painted paper and ephemera.

Supplies Needed: Glass slides, photographs printed or copied onto a transparency sheet, sheet adhesive, burnishing tool, scissors or craft knife, cutting mat

Erikia Ghumm

When Dad Was a Baby

Heritage baby photos are scanned into a computer and sized to fit the glass slide onto which they are transferred in order to create this darling spread. Because images are tiny, they are layered on top of lightly printed and stamped papers. When images are larger, they can be combined with stronger patterns without getting lost in the design. Add a swirl clip, stamps and a "typewriter key" title to the ripped and layered paper background to complete the stunning page.

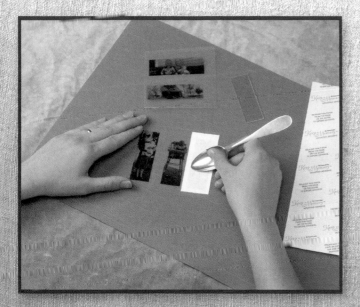

1 Print or copy photographs onto a transparency sheet. Remove one side of a sheet of adhesive and lay it on top of the image. Burnish firmly to adhere the layers. Turn over the transparency and place an other piece of sheet adhesive on top of the image. Burnish again to adhere the layers.

2 Remove the protective backing sheet to expose the adhesive layer that sits on top of the image. Lay the glass slide onto the adhesive-backed image, pressing down firmly but carefully. Burnish on the backside to adhere the layers.

3 Cut off the excess transparency sheet from around the edges of the slide with scissors or a craft knife. If using a craft knife, hold the blade at a 45-degree angle to prevent the edges from chipping.

"When crafting with glass only use pieces that have smooth or rounded edges to avoid getting cut."

Ferne

Broken and worn out vintage jewelry can be reassembled to create a "new" cherished piece which features a photograph of the loved one who once owned the adornment. This piece show-cases the image on an old optometrist lens and is layered with printed paper for an altered look.

Embellishing Photos

Decorate copies of your photographs with glitter, charms, rhinestones and other 3-D embellishments. Use one of the acid-free glues specifically designed for attaching 3-D embellishments to memory crafts. Embellished photos become works of art that make a secondary statement about the lives and times of those featured on the scrapbook pages, as well as the vision and personality of the artist.

Supplies Needed: Photographs, decorative elements such as small brads, eyelets, charms, rhinestones, buttons, scraps of paper, fake fur, velvet, bleach, inks, embossing powder, adhesives

Pamela Frye Hauer

Roadside Attractions

The Humpty Dumpty in this wild and wacky page was decorated with a multitude of items including fur eyebrows, metal dot pupils, glitter glue eyes, a paper collar, nailhead buttons and wet embossed lips. The motel sign is detailed along the edges by dragging the tip of a toothpick dipped in household bleach along the perimeter. Glitter glue and a variety of star charms and brads complete the scene. The silhouetted "Muffler Man" sports a metal hat, tiny buttons, and a belt made with a square brad and micro beads. A tiny Statue of Liberty and stamped fireworks dusted with pigment powder adorn the other "Muffler Man" photo while the dog restaurant boasts googly-eyes.

Party

The main subject has been chalked and small charms, sequins and rhinestones added to adorn the costumes on this heritage photo.

"To adhere micro beads, cut and attach double-sided sticky tape to your photo or page in the areas you wish to bead. Cover the exposed side of the tape with Micro Beads, and shake off the excess."

My Grandmother opening gifts at her Birthday & 1st Wedding Anniversary party * Oct. 27th, 1946

"For wet embossing, draw over the desired element in the photo with a glue pen, and immediately cover with embossing powder. Then, set the powder with a heat gun. Traditional photo paper can easily warp under high heat, so this technique works best on photos printed on cardstock."

Rose Lady Tin

A tin for holding small mementos is decorated with a vintage photo of a woman. Flowers and jewelry are added to the subject for a 3-D effect.

"If the glue you are using to adhere tiny design elements to your art doesn't have a fine-tipped applicator, just squeeze a little glue onto a piece of scrap paper, and use a toothpick to pick up and dot the glue where it's needed."

Photo Aging

Give photographs an aged, well-worn look by sanding them to expose the layers underneath the surface. While this technique is not suited for every photo or scrapbook page, and is absolutely not to be tried on original copies of photographs, it can add flavor to many spreads including those with an old-fashioned feel, farm, country and outdoorsy pages. It can also add power to spreads dealing with issues such as divorce and troubled times.

Supplies Needed: Photographs, sanding block with various grits

Erikia Ghumm
Photos Ken Trujillo

Brian and Erikia

The artistic studio shots of these current retro photographs take on a more realistic look when the edges are torn and sanded giving them the years of age they never saw. Layer aged photographs on top of printed papers and embellish with stickers and vintage items such as buttons.

"Create interesting effects by crumpling, inking and applying metallic rub-ons to photos that have been aged. Also try your hand at photo aging die cuts, stickers and printed materials."

1 Carefully tear along all four edges of a photograph, creating a rough perimeter. Working on a protected surface, sand the torn edges with a medium-grit sanding block. Work in varied directions until the desired effect is achieved. Once the edges are finished, complete the look by lightly sanding the entire image with a light-grit sanding block, working once again, in all four directions.

"When adhering crumpled photographs it is best to use a strong adhesive such as double sided tape or glue dots."

"Happey" Home

The photographs of the house featured on this page were taken on a drive in the country. They, as well as other elements such as the title and barbed-wire fence panoramic photograph and background papers, were aged by tearing, sanding, crumpling and inking with permanent dye ink. Other elements such as the sunflower die cuts were given the same treatment to create visual cohesion.

Tearing and Reassembling Photos

It's simple to create eye-catching distressed art by tearing up and reassembling photographs. Use copies of your pictures rather than the originals. Tear the pictures randomly, or along predetermined pattern lines. Rip them into same-size squares for the feel of a traditional mosaic, or tear them into a variety of squares and rectangles for a free-form look. Leave the ripped white photo edges in their natural state, or color them with chalks or colored pencils for a finished flair. Nestle torn pieces closely or leave margins between pieces when reassembled. The choices are up to you!

Supplies Needed: Photos, dry adhesive

Pamela Frye Hauer

"Photos of people can be torn and reassembled with interesting effects. Simply avoid tearing directly through the subject's face which creates an unseemly 'scar.'"

Dream Car

This dreamy page was created by randomly tearing a large photo of a Chevy Bellaire. The pieces were reassembled on a black mat, raw edges touching. Adhesive, applied to the centers of the torn pieces, secures them to the mat, while the edges are free to lift and curl, adding dimension to the art. A border with cropped photo tiles and a sporty car charm as well as a clever title made from tags and bottle caps in which letter stickers have been placed rounds out this racy page.

Be Happy Every Day

Diagonal tears frame a lush orange lily in this happy-go-lucky scrapbook spread. The torn photo edges are chalked before reassembling. Stickers, vellum envelopes, dried leaves, ribbon and other embellishments adorn the montage of patterned and specialty papers.

"Randomly tear photos or create pattern lines on the back of the picture along which to tear. Be sure to lay down each torn piece in its appropriate place before tearing the next piece. In other words, assemble the pieces like a puzzle as they are torn in order to prevent confusion during reassembly."

Silhouetting Photos

Silhouette cropping people, animals and objects from photographs offers creative opportunities to turn scrapbook pages into surreal works of art while eliminating background distractions and drawing the viewer's eye to the subject of the page. The best photos to use for silhouetting are in clear focus and include either full or partial body shots. Both color and black-and-white photos can be used, as can photos of all sizes from 8 x 10" to postage stamp size. Add silhouette-cropped photos to patterned, stamped and painted backgrounds for dynamic effects.

Supplies Needed: Photographs, small sharp scissors, craft knife, cutting mat

"Never silhouette crop original photos. Make copies and keep the originals safely stored away."

Erikia Ghumm

Rockabilly Rebel

The enlarged silhouette-cut photo of the guitar player on this page draws the viewer's eye, providing enormous impact for this scrapbook spread. The smaller silhouette of the motorcycle rider and other silhouetted images, including the guitar and flames, balance the spread. Decorative nailheads, charms, the "rebel" button and typewriter key title all play out the theme.

"Use a small pair of sharp, pointed scissors and a craft knife to silhouette crop photos. To adhere silhouetted images to projects, use a tape runner or a liquid glue pen."

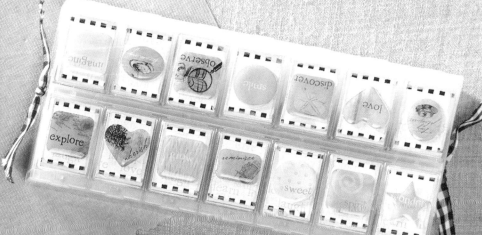

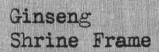

Tiny Treasures Box

This whimsical altered pill box holds an array of tiny family treasures. Epoxy stickers decorate the top of the box. Flip open a door to find a silhouetted image of a family member. The keepsake within that compartment once belonged to the person whose image is displayed. The pill box is further adorned with printed paper border stickers and acrylic paint.

Hilde

This altered bingo card ties Grandma to her favorite pastime, bingo. A transparency image, typewriter keys, beaded trim, decorative eyelets and rhinestone earrings add whimsy. Hang the piece from decorative fibers.

Ginseng Shrine Frame

A beloved family pet, sporting newly acquired wings, takes a rest on a cloud in this 3-D shrine. Tiny glass vials contain snippets of the cat's fur. Rhinestones and jewelry findings add a touch of glitter.

Mom

Turn family members into their own mini faux postage stamps. Complete the look with stamped letter stickers, torn paper and a script stamp, all aged with stamping ink for a vintage look.

Hand Coloring Photos

When a photograph is printed on traditional photo paper, only products specifically made for hand-tinting can be successfully applied to them; however, when printing photos onto white cardstock, you can hand color them with many different colorants. For best results, experiment on a copy of your photo to test the effect of the marker, chalk, colored pencil or other colorant you wish to use. Some may bleed. And each will give you a completely different effect.

Supplies Needed: Home computer and printer, white cardstock,
chalks, makeup applicators or a small soft cloth, eraser

Pamela Frye Hauer

"If you apply chalks very thickly, they tend to turn opaque over the photographic image. Simply use an eraser or adhesive pick-up square to remove excess chalk or to carefully remove mistakes."

Butch 1948

Chalks give the softest, most traditional photo-tinting look. Apply chalk to a photo with cotton swabs and blend colors with makeup applicators, a soft cloth or fingertips. You don't have to color the entire photo; try coloring just the main subject or small details. Mount the photo on a creative background. Add stamps, wrapping paper elements and other creative embellishments and journaling.

Kitty Box

Hand-tinting is not limited to black-and-white photographs. The background in this photo is altered with colored pencil dashes and red luster rub-ons, making the cat stand out from the busy background.

Utilize colored pencils to create texture on clothing and hair.

Apply metallic rub-ons with a smooth sponge for a glowing finish.

Dot the photo with gel and glitter pens for a subtle but fun look.

Use markers to outline elements, or color them in completely.

FOR ADDRESS ONLY.

FOR CORRESPONDENCE

Chapter #Three
Lettering

Just as there is an art to writing sentimental and poetic-journaling, there is an art to creating letters that are beautifully displayed. The shapes and forms of artistically created letters add to the scrapbook page design, working with other layout elements to pull together a distinct look and feel. Artistic lettering and journaling involves a plethora of materials and techniques so you don't have to have perfect handwriting to create them. In this chapter you will learn lettering techniques including:

How to manipulate letters using digital reproduction

The art of combining letters of different shapes, sizes and craft materials

The use of art materials including paints, oil pastels and scratchboard to create letters

How to apply letters to metal and glass

Stamping and embossing techniques for letters

Adding a handmade quality and artistic appeal to lettering and journaling through a flowing script written with oil pastels, chunky game piece letters or more common scrapbook supplies such as letter stickers or templates can turn a title or journaling block into a page.

Metal Stamping Letters

Journaling takes on a whole new form when incorporating words that have been hand stamped onto metal embossing foil. Metal embossing foil is an easy material with which to work because of its pliability. It can be embossed with a stylus, punched, folded and stamped upon for a variety of effects. Embossing foil can be used straight from the package or distressed by carefully crumpling, sanding, scratching or heating, which changes its color.

Supplies Needed: Metal embossing foil, steel alphabet stamps, hammer, block of wood, old scissors, paper towel, metallic rub-ons

Erikia Ghumm

Love Is a Game...

A combination of pre-stamped alphabet tags and hand-stamped words was used on this sensational page. The background was created by stamping over cardstock with watermark stamping ink, creating a tone-on-tone effect. The edges of the page were accentuated with stamping ink and rub-ons before fun embellishments of distressed playing cards, decorative netting and fibers were added. Stamped metal sentiments were adhered to the page with adhesive dots.

Time Flies

Stamping on metal offers many possibilities for projects beyond scrapbook pages because of its sturdy nature. The cover on this graphic hand-bound album features a hand-stamped title that has been punched out using a circle punch.

"For more oomph, try stamping letters at different angles. Place your stamped words in unusual places on your pages such as on top of photo mats and punched embellishments."

1 Use a piece of wood as a work surface. Cut out a piece of embossing foil and place it on the wood. Position the steel metal stamp on the embossing foil in the desired position. Grip the stamp in the middle of the handle to avoid injury. Hammer the stamp, using a solid but moderate blow. Create all the necessary letters in a similar manner until your word is complete.

2 With a ruler and an embossing stylus, mark cut lines around the completed word. Cut along the lines using an old pair of scissors. Carefully snip away sharp corners.

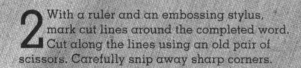

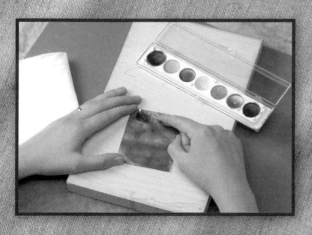

3 To enhance the appearance of the stamped letters, apply metallic rub-ons, using your finger as an applicator. Apply enough to fill in and darken the letters. Remove excess with a paper towel.

Making Scratchboard Letters

Scratchboard comes in several different colors and thicknesses and is great for creating custom lettering and journaling. The most common type of scratchboard has a black surface with a white layer beneath; however, there are other varieties of scratchboard available including white-on-white, black-over-prism and black-over-rainbow. Use a craft knife, toothpicks or an old-fashioned ink pen for scratching away the top layer on your scratchboard. There are also many wood or metal stylus tools available in craft stores that make the job simple and result in stunning journaling.

Supplies Needed: Scratchboard, alphabet stickers, templates or other letter patterns, craft knife or other sharp tool

Pamela Frye-Hauer
Photo Francine Boisclair

Papa

Scratchboard was used to create the words "Papa," "Dad" and "Father" on this tribute spread. To better understand how "Father" was created, see details on the adjacent page. To make the word "Dad," lay an alphabet template on scratchboard and trace the letters' outlines. Remove the template and scratch away the space around the letters. Chalk the exposed areas. To make the letter tiles for the word "Papa," hold an alphabet template on scratchboard while scratching out the outline of each letter. Cut out letter tiles and scuff their edges and backgrounds with a craft knife. Embellish the page with charms, torn paper, stamped images and journaling blocks.

Autumn

White scratchboard opens up many possibilities because it can be colored and stamped upon before scratching out letters or designs.

Dream

Prism scratchboard makes a dreamy title for
this journal cover. Wing-shaped charms, tiny
jewels, a vintage photo and stamped stars
complete the piece.

"The hills are a furnace of color
and mellowing light
Where junipers flame & flake,
And the blueberry dreams
like a faint blue smoke
on the height."

The Hills

Rainbow scratchboard adds a prism
of mood to journaling blocks. Colors
work well with most page designs.

*"Change the motion of your scratches
in order to create different looks.
Scratch back and forth or in little
circles, scratch away a little or a lot.
It's up to you."*

1 Lay a lettering template over a
piece of scratchboard. Using a
sharp tool such as an old fash-
ioned ink pen or toothpick, scratch
away the inside of the letter shape.

2 When completed,
carefully cut around
the letter to create a
tile. Scuff the edges of the
tile with the side of a craft
knife. Use chalks to color in
the exposed areas.

Creating Wax Resist Titles

The soft yet bold beauty of wax resists creates a stunning and unusual look for journaling. A simple stroke of an oil pastel on watercolor paper will resist a wash of watercolor paint that is applied over it. Because the oil pastels resist paint, remarkable color combinations can be achieved. Colors that would normally end up muddy, such as orange and green or yellow and purple, can be mixed with success. Experiment with this unique technique by layering several colors of oil pastels on top of one another and mixing different colors of watercolor washes to paint over the journaling.

Supplies Needed: Oil pastels, watercolor paper, watercolor paint, paintbrush, paint container, coarse salt

Erikia Ghumm

November 3 thru 13, 2001

par·a·dise (păr'a·dĭs), n. 1. [cap.] The garden of Eden. 2. Heaven. 3. A place of bliss.

Kauai, a Paradise of Beauty

The tropical feel of this vacation page was achieved with a wax resist title that runs across the top and bottom of the layout. Printed watercolor background papers draw colors from the lush greenery of the tropics and the deep blues and purples of the ocean. The Hawaiian theme is supported by the embellishments used including raffia; hula, flower and palm tree charms; silk flowers and hand-colored photo corners.

"When purchasing a pad of watercolor paper, it is best to select a 'block' pad which has its edges glued down so the paper does not warp when painted."

1 Write the page title across a sheet of watercolor paper using oil pastels.

2 Use watercolors, or mix acrylic paint and water to create a thin wash. Paint over the oil pastel writing. Sprinkle coarse salt on top of the wet paint for a mottled finish and brush off the excess when it is dry.

Photos Clara Fricke

Remembering the 1970's

The decorative title on this layout utilizes letter stickers as masks on watercolor paper. The paper was colored upon with oil pastels, the letter stickers removed and the spaces they previously occupied, painted with watercolors. Use a computer to journal. Print the journaling on patterned paper, cut and mat onto hand-drawn wax resist paper which matches the title. Complete the spread by adding texture with mesh, colored staples, a tag and velvet leaves. Create additional journaling such as the words "ME," "KIRK" and "OUR HOME" using an office label maker.

Glass Etching

Use etching cream to create subtle lettering effects on glass and mirrors for stunning page embellishments. Commercial etching creams, available in most craft stores, can be used on a multitude of small glass and mirror items such as flat glass beads, mirror and glass tiles as well as an optometrist lens for scrapbook art. Use pre-made stencils or alphabet stickers to create the style of letters you wish to etch. Or create your own letter patterns. Be sure to read all of the instructions and safety information included with the etching cream before you begin, and test it on one small item before starting your project.

Supplies Needed: Large, flat glass beads; optometrist lens; contact paper; etching cream; alphabet template or other letter pattern; small paint brush; running water supply; colored paper; craft knife

Pamela Frye Hauer

Katie

Beautifully etched glass optometrist's lens and beads create the title for this creative album page. In order to make the name more readable, the clear beads were glued with a wet, clear-drying adhesive to dark green cardstock. Torn paper, stamped images, mismatched photo corners, charms and a glass bead, under which the date is mounted, round out the page. A fiber ponytail and leaf-shaped tag add pizazz.

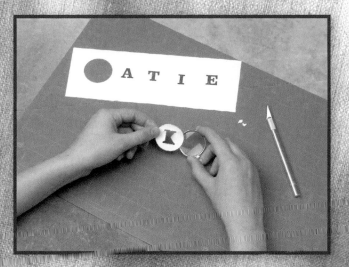

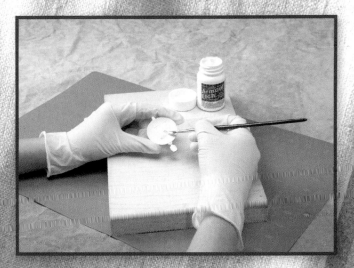

1 Create your own letters with a rubber stamp, template or pattern. Transfer the letters onto contact paper. Carefully cut them out using a craft knife. Slowly peel the backing from the contact paper and apply the sticky letter stencil to a clean glass item.

2 Wearing rubber gloves, paint a thick layer of etching cream over the letter stencil.

3 Wait the time dictated by the etching cream manufacturer. Thoroughly rinse the entire etched piece under running water. Remove the remaining stencil and dry the finished piece.

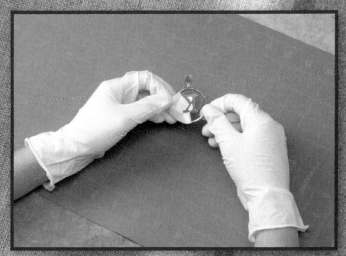

"When cutting out letters from contact paper, be sure to save any loose pieces (such as the inside triangle of the letter A). If you want the letter to be etched, these are the pieces you will apply to the glass to mask the areas. If you wish to etch the background rather than the letter, you will apply the letter itself to the glass."

Greeting Card

Use letter stickers as masks to create tiny etched tiles out of small mirrors for festive greeting cards.

"Take time before beginning your project to determine whether you wish your etched piece to feature an etched letter or whether you wish the letter to remain clear while the area surrounding it is etched. Each choice provides a different effect."

Ransom Note Journaling

Get creative with journaling by using words cut from old books, magazines, brochures, dictionaries, encyclopedias and product packaging. The search for just the right words can be almost as much fun as the creation of the scrapbook page on which they're featured. If you can't find the words you're seeking, consider using alternate words or phrases. Often, "second choices" turn out to be the most creative. If essential words are nowhere to be found, piece them together with combinations of random letters.

Supplies Needed: Vintage book, de-acidification spray, craft knife, cutting mat, liquid glue pen, tweezers

Erikia Ghumm

In the Garden

This blooming garden layout features words cut from books written about French gardens and architecture. To give this journaling structure and visual appeal, most of it is confined to the small areas of the SX-70 Polaroid photographs and the leaf-shaped tag. The journaling, serene printed paper, charms, fabric adornments, and stamping techniques pull together a well-tended look.

"Great deals can be found on old books which can supply text for ransom note journaling. Check out garage sales, flea markets and second-hand bookstores. Look for books that relate to the theme of your page in order to ensure a successful word search."

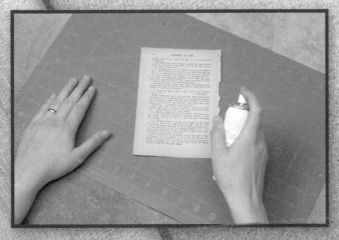

1 Text cut from books is often not archivally safe to use next to photos. De-acidify it by spraying both sides of a selected book page with a commercial de-acidifying product. Or photocopy the book page on archivally safe paper.

2 Cut selected journaling words from the book page. Arrange all the text on your scrapbook page prior to adhering. Glue down the words, using tweezers and a glue pen.

Easter

Text from the box of an egg-dying kit provided the words for these journaled tags which are colorized with green dye ink and glitter glue. The tags were mounted on patterned paper laid over mesh. Embellishments include an egg-dying loop, fibers and mini vintage postcards.

Enlarging and Distorting Letters

Customize fonts by enlarging and distorting letters on a photocopier or home scanner to turn common fonts into something much more unique. Create your text on a computer, or use alphabet stickers, rubber stamps or your own handwriting to form a word or page title. When enlarging a font from tiny to enormous, the image will distort without requiring any additional modifications for effect. Enlarged fonts can be used as a background for page elements as well as titles.

Supplies Needed: Home computer, scanner and printer or photocopy machine, white or colored paper, letter stickers, rubber stamps or a pen, scissors

Pamela Frye Hauer
Photo Francine Boisclair

France

Add something special to a dramatic page with an enlarged title word printed on white, colored or patterned paper. You may also use the enlarged word as a pattern around which you can trace, or a stencil around which you can cut, to create the word out of paper or another material. Decorate your pages with stamps, paper blocks and photocopies of travel documents.

Bigger and Bigger

Scan or photocopy text, enlarging it as much as 200 percent. Then enlarge the photocopy again and again until you reach the desired size.

FRANCE

FRANCE

FRANCE

"When using a home scanner, scan the words at a very high DPI to capture more detail and better distort the lettering. If the enlarged word won't fit onto a 8½ x 11" sheet of paper, enlarge one half of the word at a time. Piece sections together when completed."

Way Out West

Customize heritage pages by selecting and enlarging fonts that are tied to the times. Mount photos and a title inside an old children's picture book, taking advantage of the vintage background papers. Wear and tear simply add to the authenticity of the layout. Embellish with charms, stamped images and stickers.

Working With Paint Glaze

Acrylic paint glaze offers a multitude of options for creative journaling. Acrylic glazes are slow-drying paints sold in a variety of colors or non-tinted. They are used as a base and are combined with acrylic paint or other pigments for mixing custom glaze colors. A simple wash of tinted glaze across cardstock or artist weight paper is a unique base to work with for journaling. Letters can be drawn on, or lifted from, the painted background. Experiment with light papers and dark tinted glaze, or reverse the two for dramatic results.

Supplies Needed: Acrylic paint and glaze, paint palette, smooth cardstock, alphabet rubber stamps, paintbrush, stamp cleaning supplies

Erikia Ghumm
Photo Brian Ghumm

Friends Forever

An iridescent gold tinted glaze was custom mixed with teal and blue acrylic paints on this page to evoke an icy winter atmosphere. Combinations of alphabet stamps were then used to create the graphic journaling. Several layers of printed, metallic and textured papers form the background for embellishments that include metal accents, faux wax seals, dictionary definitions, and metallic rub-ons.

1 Gather materials and spread waxed paper over a work surface. Pour out a small amount of glaze onto a palette. Tint the glaze by adding a few drops of colored acrylic paint and mix slightly. Brush a thin coat of glaze onto cardstock, covering the entire piece. Using an un-inked alphabet stamp, stamp directly into the wet glaze with firm and steady pressure. Clean the stamp thoroughly after each impression with a wet paper towel or a washable stamp-cleaning pad.

Silver Xmas Tree

If you wish, forgo the alphabet stamps and journal directly into the glaze with an embossing stylus or an old pen. When using this journaling method, the glaze must be applied as you journal to achieve a clear impression. Complete the page with printed and metallic cardstock, a stamped strip, painted tags, brads, tinsel and vintage Christmas decorations.

Peace on Earth

Use paint glaze with patterned stamps to create unique backgrounds. Create the holiday greeting by reapplying glaze to a small area of the card while the card is still wet. Stamp your greeting in the newly-applied glaze.

Rainbow Embossed Journaling

Use a glue pen and several embossing powders to create beautiful multicolored wet-embossed lettering, without requiring the use of alphabet stamps. Simply lay down your chosen words formed with letter stickers, die cut or handcut paper letters or computer printed text. Trace over them with a glue pen before applying and heat-setting embossing powders.

Supplies Needed: Letter stickers, fine-point glue pen, three colors of embossing powders

Pamela Frye Hauer

Together Forever

The appeal of this vintage photo is just as strong now as when it was snapped. The lettering forming the page title was created by applying stickers directly to the page. Glue was applied over the letters before turquoise, bronze and gold embossing powders were added. While this title was made from regular embossing powders, mixing regular and ultra-thick powders can create interesting effects. Add watches and other adornments to a layered background of documents and stamped and torn papers to complete this heritage look.

1 Carefully apply letter stickers to a sheet of paper.

2 Working on one letter at a time, trace over the entire letter surface with a fine-tipped glue pen.

3 Cover remaining sections of wet glue with two or more colors of powder. Shake off the excess powder. Set the embossing powders by holding a heat gun several inches above their surface until dry.

"Don't throw away the excess embossing powder you shake off of your project. The leftover powder mixture is often beautiful. It can be used later for additional lettering or on embellishments."

Art Journal

The stamp used to create the "Art" title for this journal includes both the letters and the background patterns. To create the title effect stamp the title and background image in ink. Once the ink has dried, trace over the letters with a glue pen. Apply embossing powders to the wet glue either randomly or in a pattern. Dry the embossing powder with a heat gun and embellish the binding with a paintbrush.

Dimensional Lettering

Dimensional lettering lends itself to altered art because of its versatility. This simple lettering option allows you to form titles and journaling phrases with letter buttons and beads, letter charms, typewriter keys and other lumpy alphabet embellishments. For less complex layouts, similarly styled letters can be grouped together. On more ornate pages use letters of different shapes, styles and sizes. To create a cohesive page, choose letters that share some quality such as color, material, size or shape. You may choose to purchase letters, use vintage letters or make your own.

Supplies Needed: Metal letter charms, beads, vintage letters or other forms of dimensional letters

Love, Cherish, Adore Keepsake Box

If may be impossible to find all the vintage letters needed to complete your journaling, so create those that are missing. The lettering on this box uses cut, glued and painted balsa wood strips as well as letter stickers. Polymer clay is another great medium for creating the letters you need but can't find. Simply roll out a thin layer of polymer clay. Stamp individual letters into the clay and cut them out. Clay letters must be baked according to the manufacturer's instructions.

My Family Jewels

The boldly graphic and colorful design of this accordion album sets a perfect backdrop for dimensional lettering. While the album spans the decades and the lettering varies on each page, the album maintains a consistent look and feel because each page utilizes a single lettering style and a color palette of purples, creams and deep reds runs throughout the book.

Erika Ghumm

Roswell

Create a riotous page designed around mixed dimensional lettering. The page maintains its balance because all letters used are of similar size and all are black, white or metallic. The reflective house letters that spell out "Roswell" add drama to the page as do photographs printed onto transparency sheets, photo transfers and stamped images on printed paper. All are adhered to the background with colored staples. Adorn the page with plastic and metal charms and sparkling glitter glue.

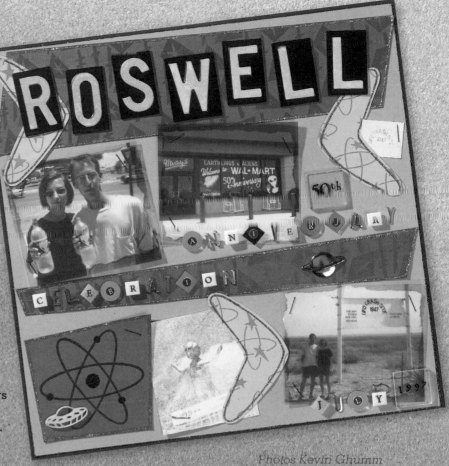

Photos Kevin Ghumm

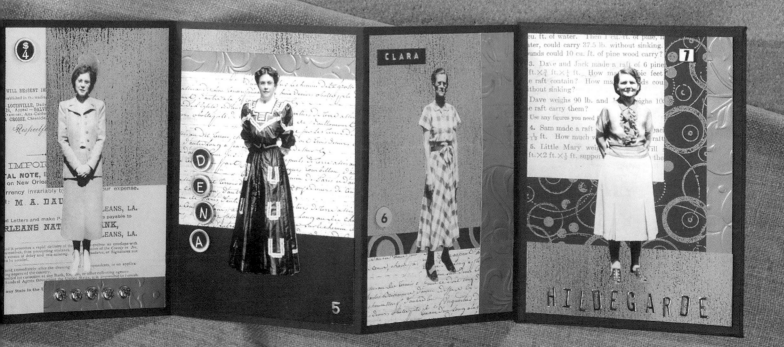

Stacking Fonts

Overlay or stack two or more letters to create limitless styles of customized titles and journaling. Clear or die-cut stickers can be used over printed, stamped, paper-cut, stenciled and most other types of letters. Stamped letters work well when placed on top of other letters, as long as the ink used is dark or opaque enough. Dark colors of pen can be used to stencil over letters printed or stamped in lighter colors. While letters in contrasting colors and value show off the most boldly, you can achieve interesting effects by layering two or more letters of similar colors for a monochromatic effect.

Supplies Needed: Sticker letters, alphabet stamps, ink pad

Pamela Frye Hauer

Hollywood

Hooray for great titles like the one featured on this California spread. The word "Hollywood" was made by layering clear sticker letters over cut out thick, stamped letters. The spread is embellished with ticket stubs, photo negatives, charms and gold frames mounted on stamped and mesh backgrounds. Tiny popcorn boxes, production slates and reels of film support the movie-loving theme.

"Try layering three letters of the same font and color, skewing them slightly for an interesting effect. Or use two letters of the same font but different colors, layering them off-register for a shadowed look. To create a sense of movement, place three or four of the same letter on top of each other, but offset each slightly to the right of the one below it."

Max

Adhere thin paper-cut letters over thick inked letters for a chunky effect. The varied letter shapes add to the frolicking feel of this album cover. Mount on the album cover and embellish with a tiny doghouse charm and stamped star.

Friends

Use a computer printer to print letters onto cardstock for a solid-looking title. Select a smaller stencil font. Place stencil directly over the computer printed letters and ink. Mount the title on a torn cardstock strip. Attach to the album and embellish with a heart charm and brads.

Baby

Place clear lowercase "pebble" stickers off-center over alphabet tiles for a look that underscores the growth from small infant to sturdy child. Mount the title on a torn paper strip and mount the strip on a background made from a book page. Embellish with stickers and a charm.

Altered Alphabet

Any project shown in this book can be applied to lettering, opening the door to an endless array of custom titles and journaling. Examples using techniques from the other chapters are shown below, plus many other fun ideas to get you started.

A-Vintage initial patch, **B**-Old jewelry pin, **C**-Alphabet stickers, printed paper, metal-rimmed tag, **D**-Wings added to a plastic letter, and mounted on a paper cloud, **E**-Vintage metal tag, **F**-Letter cut out of a collage made from magazine clippings, **G**-Vintage marquee letter, **H**-Watercolor paper painted with watercolors and a hand-drawn oil pastel letter, **I**-Letter cut from stamped craft plastic and decorated with glitter glue, **J**-Stamped tag with metal accents and a hand-drawn brush letter, **K**-Undeveloped film and letter sticker, **L**-Silhouetted photograph of a letter on a sign, **M**-Printed paper with a hand-drawn letter made with a water brush and pigment powder,

Pamela Frye Hauer & Erikia Ghumm

N-Stamped and wet embossed letter on metal mesh, mounted on paper and more mesh, **O**-Photographic tag with mesh, acrylic paint, fibers, and faux metal letter, **P**-Paper over a dimensional letter; rubbed with colored pencils, torn, and chalked, **Q**-Metal rimmed tag with vintage book page, square brad, and metal letter, **R**-Photographic rose die cut with rub-on letter, **S**-Acrylic square on top of printed paper and a cyanotype letter made with a letter sticker, **T**-Dimensional letter pressed into heated moldable foam to create a stamp, inked and stamped onto paper then cut out and mounted on transparency image, **U**-Found, **V**-Hand colored and stamped letter on faux postage stamp with stamped cancellation marks, **W**-Laminated chip with ribbon, silver leafing, and a hand-drawn calligraphy letter, **X**-Postage stamped die-cut frame over printed vellum and a stamped letter, **Y**-Stamped metal-rimmed tag with fiber, photographic flower sticker and letter sticker, **And**-Ticket with "and" postage stamp sticker, **Z**-Press type letter rubbed onto a small wood shape

Numbers-Oval tag with inked edges, ribbon and stamped numbers, **?**-Brads and nailheads attached to cardstock; cut and chalked, **!**-Three paper exclamation points of the same font; stacked skewed and mounted on transparency image and paper

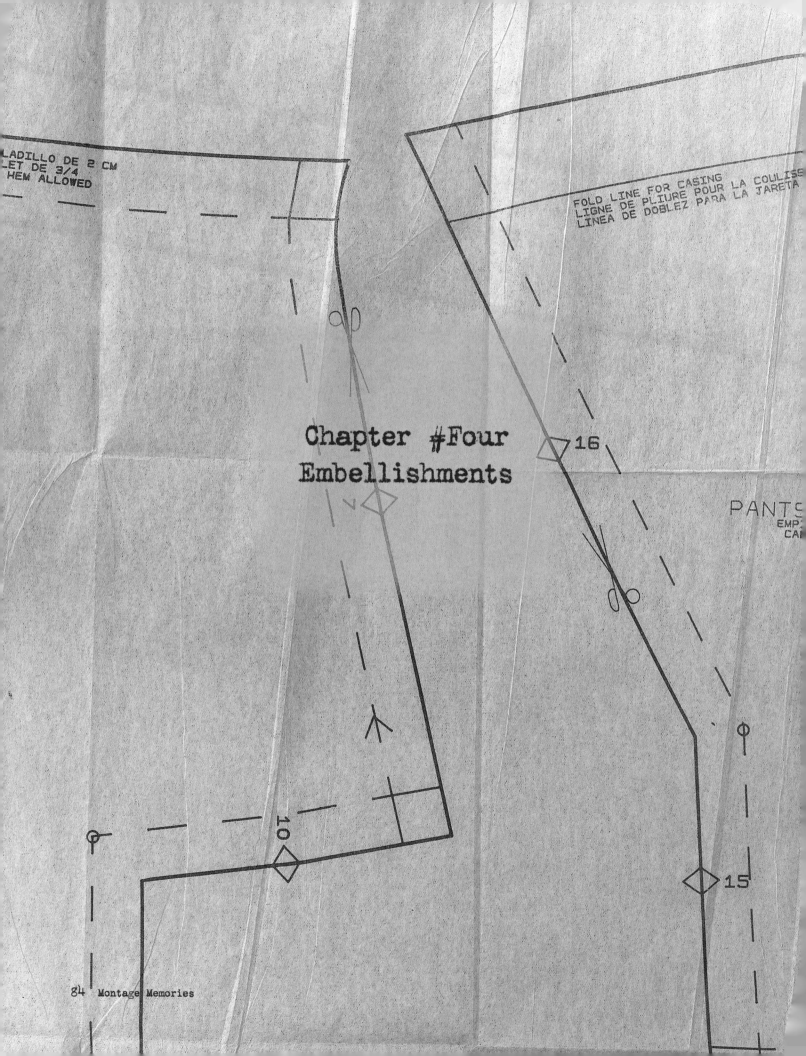

ADILLO DE 2 CM
ET DE 3/4
HEM ALLOWED

FOLD LINE FOR CASING
LIGNE DE PLIURE POUR LA COULISS
LINEA DE DOBLEZ PARA LA JARETA

16

PANTS
EMP
CA

Chapter #Four
Embellishments

10

15

Embellishments add style and interest to any scrapbook layout or memory craft project. Although embellishments are available commercially in many styles, shapes and sizes it is often fun and interesting to make your own out of unusual materials. A custom-designed and created embellishment is a fantastic way to pull together a page design and emphasize a theme, especially one that features an uncommon topic. In this chapter you will learn a wide range of techniques for making embellishments including:

How to use natural materials like plants and mica to create page adornments

Methods for utilizing metal mesh, laminate, plastic and clay in embellishing

How to make handmade paper and "vintage" paper elements

Instructions for creating your own handmade stamps

Creating your own embellishments may sound like a time-consuming project, but it can take as little or as much time as you would like to invest. The final results can be very rewarding and an expression of your individuality. Your pages will stand out as one-of-a-kind works of scrapbook art.

Decorating Laminate Chips

Laminate chip samples can be decorated in countless ways to create outstanding embellishments. These strong and sturdy "tags" can be painted, stamped, embossed, decoupaged, used as journaling blocks, turned into jewelry and much more. While laminate chips may be found at hardware stores, garage sales and thrift stores, the most reliable way to find them is to do an online search and purchase them from a laminate chip manufacturer.

Supplies Needed: Laminate chips, stamps, solvent-based ink pad, solvent-based stamp cleaner, charms, wire, needle-nose pliers, wire cutters, small drill, wood block to drill on

Erikia Ghumm

"When stamping or coloring laminate chips, keep a bottle of solvent-based stamp cleaner handy to quickly remove any mistakes from the surface."

Life Has Dealt Us a Winning Hand

Laminate chip "tags" decorated as playing cards create interesting frames for tiny Polaroid photographs in this game-themed layout. The laminate chips also provide a perfect spot for journaling created with rub-on letters and freehand script applied with an old-fashioned calligraphy dip pen. The chips are adhered to the layout with a double-sided tape which bonds to almost any surface. Brads, charms, ribbon and stamped squares embellish the heartfelt page.

Decorating With Paper

For a whimsical look, add a photographic die cut and words cut from an old book to laminate a chip. Embellish with beads, sequin and wire.

Decorating With Stickers

Dress up laminate chips with stickers. Add a finishing touch with coordinating ribbon.

Decorating With Stamping

Stamp an image on laminate chips with a solvent-based ink pad. When dry, color in with permanent craft ink markers. Adorn with an embellished brad.

Decorating With Metal

Turn a laminate chip into a funky piece of jewelry with a heart charm, decorative eyelet and ball chain. The image of the couple is a photographic transparency and the word "kiss" was created using an office label maker.

Decorating With Embossing Powder

Decorate laminate chips with paper collage images then dip them into a pot of melted ultra thick embossing powder. Or apply embossing ink to the surface of the decorated chip and cover with ultra thick embossing power. Set with a heat gun, repeating as necessary. Embellish with micro beads.

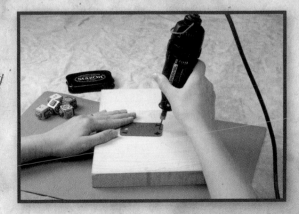

1 Stamp playing card letters and symbols in the corners of the laminate chip using a solvent-based ink pad. Allow the ink to dry. Using a small drill, make a hole in the bottom of the chip from which to hang a charm.

2 Apply the charm to the chip using wire. Finish the hole at the top with decorative eyelets, brads or ribbon.

Paper Casting

Paper casting can be used to create an endless number of original embellishments for projects with very little investment. Several companies sell supplies and kits that have everything needed to create paper casts. If you choose not to invest in a kit, you can often find items to use as paper casts around the home including candy and clay molds. You may also make your own pulp by tearing up scraps of paper and mixing them in a blender with water. Use paper casting to decorate cards or to create ornaments, decorations or gift wrap, even jewelry!

Supplies Needed: A paper molding kit or materials to create your own paper molds; materials to make paper such as recycled paper; organics including flower petals, hay, leaf sections, seeds; glitter; a blender; molds; paper towels; a straining system; colorants

"Paper castings are very porous so pens and markers may bleed which leads to unexpected (and often wonderful) effects."

"Add bits of colored paper, dried herbs, dried flower petals, mica flakes or glitter to pulp while blending it."

Pamela Frye Hauer
Photos Lester Frye

Wild Child

Purchased molds and cotton linter casting squares are used to create the casts for this exuberant page. Paper cast embellishments were chalked first, and detailed with fine-point pen for added interest. The spread's background was created with stamps and handmade paper. Corrugated cardstock, leaf buttons, charms, dried flowers and leaves and a dictionary page support the photos which have been manipulated to glow a healthy, youthful pink.

1 Tear off enough of the casting squares to cover the image on your chosen mold. Mix squares in a blender with 3 cups of water for 45 seconds. Pour into a metal mesh kitchen colander to drain.

2 Press the pulp as evenly as possible over the mold image with your fingertips. Use a sponge to press additional moisture from the pulp. When sponge no longer seems to be drawing fluid, switch to paper towels. Remove as much of the water from the pulp as possible.

3 Carefully peel the casting from the mold and lay it flat to air dry. Some molds, with the pulp still on them, can be placed in a low oven (275 degrees), for approximately 10 minutes, to speed up the drying time, (check mold manufacturer's instructions).

4 Decorate the paper castings with paint, chalk, embossing powders, pens, glitter glue or small 3-D ornaments.

Dragonfly

Copper dust glitter was added to the paper pulp when crafting this dragonfly.

Leaf

Bits of green paper were added when blending the pulp for the casting of the leaf.

Adorning Paper Frames

In days gone by, studio portraits were beautifully displayed in embossed, die-cut paper frames of all sorts of sizes and shapes. Most commonly found in cream, brown, gray, or black, they ran the gamut from plain to elaborate. You can often find old frames at garage sales or thrift and antique stores. You may even have a relative who owns a pile and will allow you to "adopt" a few. When adorning paper frames, the sky is the limit. Try adding charms, punched pieces or ephemera, or stamping, painting or coloring your frame in other ways.

Supplies Needed: Vintage portrait studio frames, various embellishments and colorants

Erikia Ghumm

Eldon

The paper frame on this heritage page features the original photograph that came with it. To alter the frame for the scrapbook page, the folding sides which were intended to act as a stand were cut and removed. Nailheads, eyelets and key charms in various metallic colors along with other metallic accents were added to create a manly look. The carefully chosen journaled statement speaks poetically to the adventures awaiting the young man in the portrait.

Hunter

Decorative paper frames work as well with modern photographs as heritage photos. This 1960s-style paper frame assumes a modern look with the addition of punched and stamped paper, a metal-rimmed tag, a dog bone and letter charms. A touch of color added to the inner frame opening creates a bright contrast to the dog's dark fur. The silhouette-cropped photo is layered on top of a printed transparency for visual interest.

"When adhering frames with hanging embellishments such as charms and tags to a scrapbook layout, use dimensional foam adhesive. This will allow the swinging elements to hang freely."

Brian and Erikia

Go over the top by turning a plain paper frame into an elaborate work of art. Vintage beads and buttons are meticulously placed on this frame with eye-catching effects. The decorative element was created by stringing beads and then laying them on the frame on top of a thin line of liquid glue. Once the design was completed, a light coat of gel medium was painted over it to act as a sealer. The date and other journaling was included opposite the photograph.

Photo Ken Trujillo

Creating With Craft Plastic

Create glamorous accents for your scrapbook pages with clear craft plastic, rubber stamps and glitter glue. Craft plastics and acetates vary in weights. Some are acid-free, making them safe to use next to photos. Use solvent inks to stamp designs on plastic. Most pigment and dye inks will not dry completely and will smear. Be creative when selecting the final punched shape of your embellishment. There are hundreds of designs available to suit every page theme.

Supplies Needed: Craft plastic, solvent ink pad, glitter glue writers, frame and design stamps, punches, marker, scissors or craft knife, clear-drying wet adhesive, dimensional adhesive dots

Pamela Frye Hauer

"If you don't feel like stamping, or can't find the design you desire, use your computer and printer to print patterns directly onto craft plastic. Several manufacturers sell plastic designed for this purpose."

Jeannie

Glamour exudes from this rich spread. Framed faces and flowers made from craft plastic are decorated with touches of glitter for a glitzy effect. Checkers, a feather and charms mix company with velvet and patterned papers in ruby reds and shades of pink. Create the "woman's face embellishment" and "flower" embellishments by following the instructions on the adjacent page. Then adhere the finished "face" pieces to the spread with clear adhesive. Attach the flowers with dimensional adhesive dots over a poetic journaling block and matted photo.

1 To create the decorative faces featured on the "Jeannie" spread, use black solvent ink to stamp a frame stamp onto a piece of plastic. Press firmly.

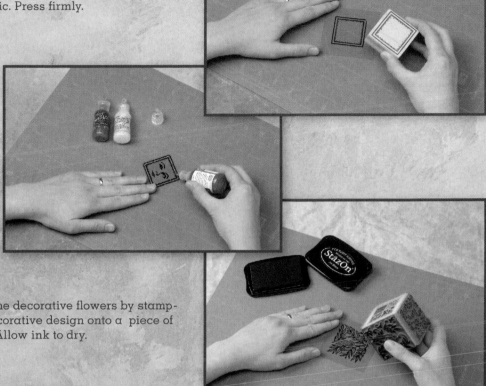

2 Inside the stamped frame image, stamp a face design. Allow the images to dry thoroughly. When dry, cut out the frame with scissors or a craft knife and decorate with glitter writers.

3 Create the decorative flowers by stamping a decorative design onto a piece of plastic. Allow ink to dry.

4 Punch the stamped design with a flower-shaped punch. Decorate with glitter. Create the smaller flower in a similar manner. Color the unstamped side of the flower with a permanent red marker and a glitter glue center.

Las Vegas Picture Frame

To create this fun-loving frame, stamp tiger stripes and print the zig zag pattern onto plastic. Use a circle punch to cut out multiple shapes. Adorn the circles with gold glitter and charms. Attach the decorated circles to your frame with 3-D self-adhesive dots.

Making Handmade Stamps

Use moldable foam and metal charms to make one-of-a-kind stamps. Several companies make foam sheets that can be heated and then molded. The sheets are available in varying thicknesses and are very easy to cut with scissors or a sharp craft knife. The array of charms available open up hundreds of possible designs that will work with pages from rowdy to romantic.

Supplies Needed: Pencil, scissors or craft knife, metal ruler, moldable foam sheets, metal charms, heat gun

Pamela Frye Hauer

Cowboy Up

An assortment of cowboy-themed stamps was created to embellish this high-energy cowboy spread. The background paper was stamped with a wood-grain rubber stamp. Stamped horses, boots and a cowboy hat form a loose border across the bottom of the pages. A cropped border of rodeo moments runs across the top.

"Thicker sheets of foam are almost an inch and a half thick. If you want your stamp to have a curvy outline, you may find it difficult to cut the desired shape from this dense material, so use thinner stock for these projects. If you find it difficult to stamp cleanly with a thinner foam stamp, glue a piece of cut foam core to the back of the stamp to stiffen it."

Western Union

Avoid having to cut foam shapes to create stamps by purchasing one of the many precut shapes of moldable foam available. Foam stylus tips are available in many designs too, and work well to help impress the smaller details on delicate charms, such as the flower used on this card. Embellish with tickets, and the original charm used to create the stamp.

1 Cut moldable foam into a rectangle slightly larger than the charm you plan to use. To do this, lay the foam sheet on a cutting surface. Use a metal ruler and craft knife to cut the foam. Use the same knife to nick the edges of the foam block to give the stamp a rugged look.

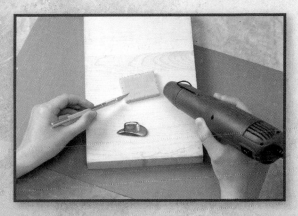

2 Heat the foam block with a heat gun for about 30 seconds. Be sure to keep moving the heat gun to avoid overheating the foam in one spot.

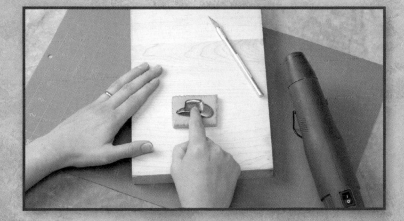

3 Quickly place the charm facedown onto the heated block and press it firmly into the foam. Hold the charm in place about 20 seconds until the block starts to cool. Use a tip of a pencil or other tool to depress small details.

4 When the foam has cooled, remove the charm. The foam stamp is now ready to be used like any other stamp. Ink it with pads, stamp markers or paint. Stamp the image directly onto your artwork or onto paper and cut it out.

Mica Tile Transfers

Mica is a transparent mineral that can be carefully separated into very thin pieces. It comes in various shapes and in sizes up to 8 x 10". Mica can be used for a multitude of stamping, decoupage, and layering techniques. Because it is transparent, it is also a great material for image transfers. Transferring images onto mica tiles is an easy technique that creates complex-looking images with worn and aged appeal. Mica transfers can be attached to layouts, album covers and memory boxes using gel medium, brads, eyelets, staples and stitching.

Supplies Needed: Mica, gel medium, inkjet copies of clip art, burnishing tool, paintbrush, waxed paper

Erikia Ghumm

Beadazzling

Creating a unique garden-themed layout in an altered book is easy with the addition of mica tile transfers. The garden illustrations used on the mica tiles are drawn from a vintage illustrated children's dictionary and pieces of vintage wallpaper. Colored staples are used for quick attachment of the tiles. This layout also features manipulated SX-70 Polaroid photographs, stamped vintage seam binding tape, metal accents, mesh paper, fiber and acrylic paint.

"When making mica tile transfers, create several copies of clip art images with which to experiment."

Art and Soul

The magical illusion on this card was crafted with a soulful touch. The bottom layer of the card is made up of a plain white shipping tag which has been stamped and embellished with transparent stickers. The tag is overlaid with a sheet of printed vellum. The final layer of the card is made of a mica tile with a photographic transfer. The mica transfer is attached to the tag with machine stitching before the word "soul" was stamped and embossed.

Photo Ken Trujillo

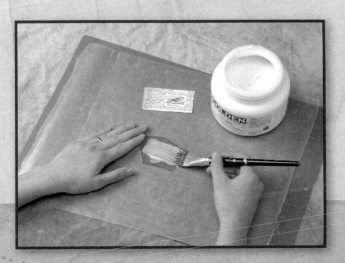

1 Lay a sheet of waxed paper over your work area. Brush an even coat of gel medium onto a piece of mica tile. Quickly place the mica tile facedown on an inkjet-printed image. Press down the tile, making sure it is in complete contact with the image.

2 Allow the image to set for about 20 seconds to moisten the paper. Flip the tile over and quickly but firmly burnish the backside while carefully holding the image in place.

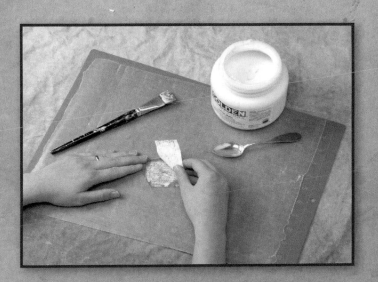

3 Carefully and slowly begin to peel up the paper, exposing the image that has been transferred to the tile. If a mica layer is stuck to the paper, separate it and hold it down while removing the paper. Or peel it away from a different area. Finish with a thin, even coat of gel medium.

Embellishing With Clay

The versatility of polymer clay makes it a perfect medium for scrapbooks, memory crafts and altered art. It comes in a variety of colors and textures. Creating embellishments with polymer clay is easy and relatively inexpensive. Just remember that the tools used for crafting clay embellishments should never be used for food preparation or storage. Experiment with creating flat, dimensional, sculpted and textured embellishments. Because these handcrafted embellishments are sturdy after being baked, they work well as decorations for album covers, memory boxes, and 3-D assemblages.

Supplies Needed: Polymer clay, brayer or clay-dedicated pasta machine, stamps, stamping ink, templates, clay knife, clay scraper, smooth tile

Erikia Ghumm

Floyd W. Miller

Egyptian-themed embellishments are difficult to find ready-made, but they can be handmade and in doing so, you control the style, shape and colors, assuring that they coordinate with other page elements. For an authentic Egyptian look, combine stamped and printed papers that have been crumpled, inked, and burned, along with a rubbing of a textured purse. Collage these pieces inside of a raised, printed frame and add a photo printed on canvas. Embellish with tags, charms and fibers.

"To adhere handcrafted polymer clay embellishments to layouts, use a dot adhesive or double-sided tape. These adhesives also work well for adhering textured and crumpled papers to a background. For adhering clay embellishments to album covers and other memory craft art, use a thick silicone adhesive."

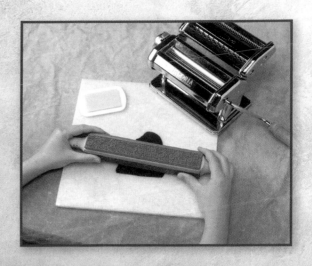

1 Condition a piece of polymer clay by kneading it until it becomes pliable. Roll the clay out in a sheet until it is approximately 1/16" thick using a clay-dedicated pasta machine or a brayer. Ink a stamp with clear embossing ink and press the stamp into the rolled out clay.

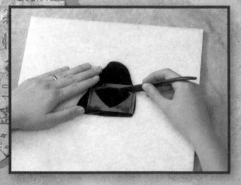

3 Rub an ink pad over the textured surface of the stamped clay piece. This will highlight the raised areas. Create a second stamped and cut piece, using a different color of clay and layer the pieces together. When complete, bake according to manufacturer's instructions.

2 Use a template to cut the previously stamped piece of clay into your chosen shape.

Gaiety Girl Journal

Polymer clay is a durable material that can be used on a variety of projects such as this distinctive journal cover. A handmade tag and purchased charms dress up this cover with a cheerful style.

Combining Elements

Combine small crafting embellishments into recognizable objects to adorn your scrapbook pages. This fun project is the perfect way to utilize odds and ends from your embellishment bins. Once you start stretching your imagination, you're sure to find uses for just about anything you've got on hand including eyelets, brads, nailheads, tags, photo corners, jewelry findings and hardware such as nuts, bolts and washers. Spread the embellishment supplies in front of you and play until recognizable objects such as faces, bugs and flowers take shape.

Supplies Needed: Assorted paper and metal tags, eyelets, brads, nailheads, jewelry findings, small game pieces and other found objects, assorted sizes of adhesive dots, clear-drying wet adhesive

Pamela Frye Hauer

Lucky Cat

Small round paper tags colored with metallic rub-ons or chalks form the heads of the classy cats on this page. Copper and brass tags form noses and cheeks while eyelets, beads and googly eyes round out the faces. Once dried, the faces were mounted on a border strip and photos, metal letters, a hand lettered title and journaling were added to finish off this purrrfect page.

"Experiment with adhesives until you find the one that works with the materials you want to attach. Small metal pieces are generally easy to attach with mini adhesive dots, while wood and paper pieces adhere better with a wet adhesive."

Flower Album Cover

Create a one-of-a-kind album cover by creatively piecing together small embellishments. This sturdy flower makes a strong statement, sprouting in the center of a green album shadow box.

1 Use your finger to apply metallic rub-ons to the white center of a metal-rimmed tag. Mix and match found objects until you determine just the right "face" for your cat.

2 Attach found objects to tag using a clear-drying wet adhesive. Set your cat aside to dry before attaching it to scrapbook page.

Nature Printing

The beauty of nature is captured on a scrapbook page with prints made with real plant leaves and flowers. Plants can be gathered from around the house, from a flower bouquet or in your yard or a park. When choosing leaves or flowers for printing, look for sturdy well-textured plants. Heartier plants may be able to be used for several prints and will provide the best outcome.

Supplies Needed: Acrylic paint, paint palette, cosmetic sponges, newsprint, tweezers, fresh plant leaves and flowers, smooth cardstock

*Erikia Ghumm
Photos Brian Ghumm*

Enduring Friendship

"Good plants to use for nature printing projects:
rose leaves, geranium leaves
ivy leaves, sage leaves
dusty miller leaves
cosmos flowers, pansy flowers
and baby breath flowers."

Nature print embellishments add a special touch to this page which showcases a photo of best friends in a garden setting. For an interesting effect, experiment by printing with different colors of paint such as the nontraditional colors of purple and chartreuse used with the dusty miller leaf on this page. The stamped leaf embellishments, photo and journaling blocks were mounted on a background which includes a dictionary definition of "Leafage" and delicate but sturdy mesh paper. Stamps, paper clips and a tiny tag round out the page.

1 Gather fresh plant leaves and flowers. Press them between heavy books for approximately 15 minutes. Create a paint palette from waxed paper. Lay out several paint colors. Lightly dab a cosmetic sponge into the paint. Use the sponge to lightly apply ink to the pressed leaf or flower.

2 Carefully place the inked plant material onto the cardstock, using tweezers if necessary. Cover the plant with a sheet of newsprint and press gently. Carefully remove the newsprint and use tweezers to lift off the inked plant material.

"Ink the veined underside of leaves and the tops of flowers for the most dramatic results."

Sheri and Tasha

Nature printing takes on a sleek look when plant materials like cosmos flowers are printed onto black cardstock with off-white ink. A monochromatic color scheme such as this works particularly well with black-and-white photographs. Embellish with brads and a chunky button title.

Embossing Metal Mesh

Stamp and wet-emboss onto metal mesh for one-of-a-kind embellishments. Metal mesh, sold in folded sheets or rolls, specifically for use in art projects, is available in many colors and screen sizes. It can be used to create jewelry, ornaments and boxes as well as great embellishments for scrapbooks. Mesh can be easily cut with scissors (use an old pair to avoid dulling new blades). It is pliable enough to shape with fingertips—however, cut edges can be sharp so work with care.

Supplies Needed: Scissors, metal mesh sheets, rubber stamps, embossing ink pad, ultra thick embossing powder, heat gun, dry adhesive, wet adhesive

Pamela Frye Hauer

Where Loveliness Is Found

Create an assortment of fall leaf embellishments using metal mesh and different colors of embossing powders. Adhere the leaves to the page with clear wet adhesive or double-sided tape. Layer leaves for dimension, applying a solid weight on top until the adhesive is dry. Finish the page with rubber-stamped images, brad stickers and other embellishments.

"If the stamp being used has small details, they will not be visible in the finished piece, so be sure to pick stamps that have bold and recognizable outlines."

You Hold the Key

For a different look cut a wide block of mesh around a stamped and embossed image (rather than cutting out the stamped and embossed shape's silhouette). Leave the edges as they are, or fold them over to form a frame. You may also wish to cut around half of the image, bending the cut portion while leaving the uncut portion to lie flat.

1 To create wire mesh autumn leaves, cut a piece of fine screen slightly larger than the stamp you wish to use. Select a stamp. Using a pigment ink pad, stamp one leaf onto the cut piece of mesh.

"Warning! While heating the embossing powder, hold the mesh with a tool such as a craft knife, instead of your fingers. The mesh can become very HOT!"

2 Quickly cover the wet ink with copper ultra thick embossing powder and set it with a heat gun. Repeat steps one and two using a different color of ultra thick embossing powder.

3 Use scissors or a craft knife to carefully cut around the outline of each leaf.

4 Shape bottom leaf and mount on scrapbook page. Layer second leaf on top, for added dimension.

Supplies for Featured Art

Page 6
Secondhand Sisters
Paper/DMD/Magenta, Clippings/Wonderland Emporium/found, Pattern stamp/Paper Candy, Flower stamp/Magenta, Cherry stamp/Duncan, Tiger print stamp/Rubber Stampede, Frame stamp/Hero Arts, Acrylic squares/Magenta, Glitter glue/Ranger, Scratchboard/Canson, Letter patterns (for Sister on scratchboard)/S and E-Creative Imaginations/I-Ma Vinci's Reliquary/Making Memories, R/Colorbok, Rhinestones/Jewel Craft, Receipt, Bingo card, ephemera/found/vintage

Pages 8-9
Tools
Small hammer/Magic Scraps, Metal ruler/C-Thru Ruler, Mini stapler/Swingline, Scissors/Fiskars, Craft knife/Xacto by Hunt Corp., Piercing tool/Making Memories, Wood stylus/AMACO, Needle-nose pliers/unknown, Eyelet setter/Making Memories, Hole punch/Making Memories, Needles/vintage, Brayer/vintage, Sandpaper/Norton

Adhesives
Glue pen/EK Success, Tab applicator/Hermafix, Tape runner/Hermafix, Silicone adhesive/E6000, Wet adhesive/USArtQuest, Glue dots/Glue Dots Intl.

Colorants
Colored pencils/EK Success, Paint pen/Ranger, Calligraphy ink/Dr. Ph.Martin's, Acrylic paint/Golden Artists Colors, Fine point pen/Sakura, Photo tinting pen/EK Success, Dual-tipped marker/EK Success

Applicators
Dusting brush/Toybox, Stylus tip stamp/Clearsnap, Paintbrushes/unknown, Sea sponge unknown, Brush sponge/Inkadinkado, Comb/Plaid, Ink pen/vintage

Stamping
Block pattern stamp/JudiKins, Design stamp/Club Scrap, Object (key) stamp/Worsdworth, Label stamp/Limited Edition Rubberstamps, Roller stamp/Clearsnap

Stamping Colorants
Pigment rainbow ink pad/Clearsnap, Metallic rub-ons/Craf-T, Black felt ink pad/Ranger, Colored dye ink pad/Ranger, Embossing powder/Ranger, Embossing embellishments/Ranger, Pigment powder/Ranger

Chemicals
Stamp pad cleaner/Ranger, Adhesive remover/un-du, De-acidification spray/EK Success, UV inhibitor/EK Success

Page 10-11
Supplies
Game pieces/Queen of Tart/vintageStamps/Toybox, Eyelets, snaps, nailheads, spiral clips/JewelCraft/Limited Edition Rubberstamps/Doodlebug Design, Photo corners/Canson/vintage, Tinsel/Magic Scraps, Labels/ARTchix Studio/Limited Edition Rubberstamps/Collage Joy/vintage, Bottle caps/

vintage, Tags/DMD/Limited Edition Rubberstamps/Ma Vinci's Reliquary, Seam binding, thread/vintage, Charms/Boutique Trims/ARTchix Studio/Limited Edition Rubberstamps/Art Sanctum/vintage, Buttons/vintage, Fibers/Art Sanctum, Keys, Optometrist lenses/ARTchix Studio/vintage, Playing cards/vintage Ephemera, clip art, reproduction photographs, etc./ARTchix Studio/Limited Edition Rubberstamps/Club Scrap/FoofaLa/Queen of Tarts/ARTitude Zine/vintage

Pages 12-13
Customizing Pre-made Albums

Decorated Tin With Scrapbook Necklace
Printed papers, Mini scrapbook, Faux wax seal, Rub-on letters/Creative Imaginations, Adhesive/Therm O Web, Glitter/Stampendous, Tin/Ranger, Ball chain/American Tag Co.

Accordion Album (Hall)
Album/Kolo, Colored metal glass top tin lid/American Science and Surplus, Wing sticker/NRN, Bitty beads/Club Scrap, Craft ink/Dr. Ph. Martin's, Photo paper/Epson

Erikia's Scrapbook 12 x 12" Post-Bound Album
Album/Pioneer, Tag/American Tag Co., Stamp, letter stickers/Club Scrap, Stamping ink/Clearsnap, Label maker/DYMO, Ribbon/Wal-Mart

Memories 12 x 12" Post-Bound Album
Album/Pioneer, Typewriter keys/Creative Imaginations, Silk fabric/vintage

Dream, Art, Create 11 x 14" Hidden Spiral-Bound Album
Album/Canson, Pewter circle and square letters, eyelet letters, eyelet tag letters, metal word/Making Memories, Wire word/Creative Imaginations, Nailhead letters/JewelCraft, Metal foil/AMACO, Steel letter stamps/Young Bros. Stamp Works, Inc./Harbor Freight, Metallic rub-ons/Craf-T, Acrylic paint/Golden Artist Colors, Glitter glue/Ranger

B&W Photographs
Album/Canson, Typewriter keys/ARTchix Studio, Conchos/Boutique Trims, Dimensional glue/JudiKins, "&" stamp/Hero Arts, Stamping ink/Tsukineko, ribbon/Offray, Game letters/vintage

Tag Book Album (Memories)
Tag book/Rubba Dub Dub, Printed paper/Magenta, Keyhole stamp/Wordsworth, Images/ARTchix Studio, Word stamps/Limited Edition Rubberstamps, Shadow stamps/Hero Arts

Pages 14-15
Little Fashion Book
Album kit/Magenta, Woman and buttons/found/vintage, Twine/The Robin's Nest

Pets Album
Paper/DMD, Alphabet stamps/Ma Vinci's Reliquary, Puzzle pieces/found

Travel Journal
Cover and discs/Rollabind, Images/Stampa Rosa, Pattern stamp/Clearsnap

8 Ball Box
Round box/unknown, Tiger print stamp/Rubber Stampede, Embossing powder/Ranger, Mirror, 8 ball, and dice-found/vintage

Dog Shadow Box
Shadow box/unknown, Clip art/Dover, Buttons/JHB International, Charms and figurines/found/vintage, Fibers/EK Success, Stamps/All Night Media

Hand-Bound Tag Album (Explore)
Tags/American Tag Co., Laminate/Therm O Web, Slide mount/Loersch, Copper tape/USArtQuest, Printed transparency/ARTchix Studio, Ribbon/Offray, Book page/vintage

Hand-Bound Album (Junque)
Loose leaf rings/ACCO, Decorative eyelets, typewriter keys, printed paper, spray adhesive/Creative Imaginations, Paint by numbers/vintage

Tobacco Tin With Accordian-Fold Pages
Photo of woman, mini rose postcard/ARTchix Studio, Postcard sticker/NRN, Stamp/Limited Edition Rubberstamps, Stamping inks, moldable stylus, textured mat/Colorbox by Clearsnap, Rhinestones/JewelCraft, Matte acrylic sealer/Plaid

Altered Book (Tide Pools & Beaches)
Book, reproduced postcard/vintage, Stamping inks/Ranger, Nailhead letters/JewelCraft, Metal foil/AMACO, Steel letter stamps/Young Bros. Stamp Works, Inc., Metallic rub-ons/Craf-T, Photo corners/3L

Pages 18-19
Brayer Painting
Mother Sweet as a Rose
Craft ink, Calligraphy ink /Dr. Ph. Martin's, Pen/Sakura, Brayer/Speedball, Nailhead letters, Sequins, Seed beads/JewelCraft, Stamps/Clearsnap, Inkadinkado/Fruit Basket Up Set, Tag/American Tag Co., Rose die cut/Paper House Productions, Love epoxy sticker/Creative Imaginations, Cherish sticker/Stampendous, Perfume label/Limited Edition Rubberstamps, Jute/Magic Scraps, Photo paper/Epson, Rose postage stamp, Balsa wood strips, Calligraphy dip pen

Soar
Card/DMD, Transparency/Epson, Acrylic paint/Golden Artist Colors, Stamp/Stampin' Up!, Stamping ink/Tsukineko, Word sticker/Stampendous, book page/vintage

Pages 20-21
Masking Words and Images
Look for a Starfish
Book/Vintage, Inks/Ranger, Application sponge/Ranger, Vellum/DMD, Adhesive/Therm O Web, Starfish stamp/Hero Arts, Number stamps/Stamp Craft by Plaid, Stamping inks/Ranger, Printed paper/Creative Imaginations, Pen/American Crafts, Mermaid Charms/ARTchix Studio, Eyelets/JewelCraft, Wire/Artistic Wire, Metal foil/AMACO, Steel letter stamps/Young Bros. Stamp Works Inc., Metallic rub-ons/Craf-T, Paper clip/Cavallini and Co.

Pages 22-23
Scanning and Copying Images
JHH
Fibers/Rubba Dub Dub, Eyelets- Magic Scraps, Ink/Tsukineko, Ephemera: Scrabble tiles, stamp, Basketball and football-found/vintage scanned object Samples Images/vintage

Pages 24-25
Inking Embossed Paper
The Cunning Cat
Embossed paper and frame/K & Company, Cardstock/DMD, Paper crimper/Fiskars, Letter template/Wordsworth, Label maker/DYMO, Stamping inks/Ranger, Fibers/Art Sanctum, Ribbon/The Robin's Nest, Metal charm/ARTchix Studio, Steel letter stamps/Harbor Freight Tools, Metallic Rub-Ons/Craf-T

Memories of Grandma Ann box and tuck-away Album
Book Box/USArtQuest, Hand bound album/Rollabind, Specialty paper/All Night Media/Club Scrap, Embossed sticker/K & Company, Stamping ink/Ranger, Stamp/Limited Edition Rubberstamps, Label maker/DYMO, Decoupage medium/Plaid

Pages 26-27
Laminating Layers
Live, Love, Laugh
Laminating sheets/Therm O Web, Papers/All Night Media/Magenta, Stamps/JudiKins, Magenta, Tinsel/Magic Scraps, Confetti/Ranger, Word stickers/Stampendous, Metal words/Creative Imaginations, Charms/Boutique Trims/Magenta, Fibers/Magic Scraps, Paper hearts/EK Success, Tiny hearts/Limited Edition Rubberstamps, Eyelet stickers/Stampendous, Cigar band/Queen of Tarts, Velvet heart and fortunes/vintage

Pages 28-29
Using Clip Art
I Swallowed a Bowling Ball
Album/Rollabind, Printed papers/Karen Foster Design/Magenta, Clip art/Dover, Pattern stamps/JudiKins/Magenta, Bowling ball stamp/Clearsnap, Small bowling images/vintage, Alphabet stamps/Close To My Heart/River City Rubberworks, Typewriter letters/FoofaLa, Inks/Ranger, Charms/Boutique Trims

Clip art Samples
Clip art/Dover

Pages 30-31
Making Handmade Paper
A Surprise Bouquet
Papermaking kit, dried flower petals/Arnold Grummer, Mesh paper/Creative Imaginations, Reproduction ephemera, ribbon, trim, woven label/Me and My Big Ideas, Charms/Boutique Trims, Paper clip/ Cavallini and Co., Photo paper/Epson, Words cut from book/vintage, Dried flower petals/from bouquet

Pages 32-33
Creating a Decoupage Collage
The Foreigner
Printed Paper/Paper Adventures, Antique decoupage finish/Plaid, Flower and text clippings/vintage, Daisy pattern unknown, Rolling pattern stamp/Clearsnap, Frame stamp/JudiKins, Metal flowers/JHB International, Beads/JewelCraft

Time Flies
Album/Canson, Clock and text clippings/found/vintage, Antique decoupage finish/Plaid, Writing stamp/Limited Edition, Mesh/Magic Scraps, Wings/Rubber Baby Buggy Bumpers, Mulberry paper/DMD, TIME letters/Club Scrap, Square alphabet beads/Limited Edition Rubberstamps/unknown, Clock stamp/River City Rubberworks, Nameplate and eyelets/Magic Scraps, Alphabet stamps/Hero Arts, Press type/ChartPak, Tags/American Tag/Hot Off The Press/found, Ink/Clearsnap, Embossing powder/Ranger

Pages 34-35
Making Faux Mosaics
Best Friends
Printed and metallic papers/Paper Adventures, Stamps/JudiKins/Clearsnap, Stamping inks/Clearsnap, Sheet adhesive and dot adhesive/Therm O Web, Sand and glitter "grout"/Magic Scraps, Letter stickers, epoxy word stickers, and faux wax seals/Creative Imaginations, Inkjet canvas/Marshall's

The Eriksen Family 1970s
Clock/No Boundaries, Printed transparencies/Magic Scraps, Silver leaf/USArtQuest, Sheet adhesive/Therm O Web, Pop dots/Stampin Up!, Photo paper/Epson

Pages 36-37
Cutting Stencils
My Baby Blue
Blue sparkle cardstock/DMD, Vellum/NRN, Silver textured papers/Paper Adventures, Vintage bingo card/Queen of Tarts, Vellum envelope/Ma Vinci's Reliquary Star templates/C-Thru Ruler, Hot Off The Press, Alphabet stamps/Hero Arts, Word sticker/Stampendous, Computer fonts/Canterbury/Harting/Prestige Elite, Charms/Boutique trims, Blue stars/Limited Edition Rubberstamps

Memories
Album/Kolo, Sparkly blue paper/Paper Adventures, Memories stamp/Limited Edition Rubberstamps, Man stamp/Paper Candy, Pattern stamp/JudiKins, Inks/Ranger, Embossing powder/Ranger, Glitter glue/Ranger, Charm/found

Pages 40-41
Transferring Photos Onto Laminate
Florida, a Journey
Book/vintage, Patterned paper/EK Success, Laminate/Therm O Web, Adhesive/Therm O Web, Metallic Rub-ons/Craf-T, Stamping inks/Ranger, Alphabet stamps/Stamp Craft by Plaid, Nautical stamps/Club Scrap, Tag, wire word, epoxy sticker/Creative Imaginations, Paper clips/Cavallini and Co., Mini Scrabble tiles/Limited Edition Rubberstamps, Book pages/vintage

Pages 42-43
Creating Photo Montages
King of the Hill
Vintage paper ephemera/Collage Joy/Queen of Tarts, Compass and clock stickers/NRN, "Memories" tile/Creative Imaginations, Tiny Scrabble letters/Limited Edition Rubberstamps

Montage samples
Photos/modern/vintage

Pages 44-45
Printing Cyanotypes
Photo Shoot
Cyanotype paper/Nature Print Paper, Album/Canson, Printed paper/Wordsworth, Metal embellishments and tags/Making Memories, Slide mounts/Loersch, Fibers/EK Success, Tag rub-ons/Creative Imaginations, Hand colored photo corners/Canson, Stamping ink/Clearsnap, White pen/Sakura

The Hall Family Accordion Album
Album/Kolo, Cyanotype paper/Nature Print Paper, Tags/DMD, Stickers/Creative Imaginations, Stamps/River City Rubber Works/Hero Arts, Stamping ink/Ranger, Collage ephemera/Artchix Studio/Limited Edition Rubberstamps, Calligraphy ink/Dr. Ph. Martin's, Fibers/Rubba Dub Dub

Pages 46-47
Printing on Alternative Surfaces
Midnight
Cardstock and handmade paper/DMD, Wood printed paper/Hot Off The Press, Dog clip art/Dover, Alphabet stickers/Creative Imaginations, Blue image/ARTchix Studio, Animal quote stamp/Wordsworth, Paw stamp/All Night Media, Background stamp/Clearsnap, Purple and blue ink/Fiber Scraps, Fibers/Fiber Scraps, Ribbon/ARTchix Studio, Dog charm/vintage

Printing on Specialty Paper Samples
Mulberry paper/DMD, Velvet paper/Magenta, Canvas/Tara Materials, Shrink plastic/Grafix, Book page and paper bag/found

Pages 48-49
Transferring Photos Onto Glass
When Dad Was a Baby
Printed paper, border sticker, panoramic photograph/Creative Imaginations, Embossed paper/K & Company, Typewriter keys, reproduction baby photos/ARTchix Studio, Number cut outs/FooFaLa, Stamp/Love to Stamp, Stamping ink/Ranger, Glass slides/American Science Surplus, Sheet adhesive/Therm O Web, Transparency sheet, photo paper/Epson, Photo tinting dyes/Marshall's, Paper clips/Wal Mart, Cavallini and Co., Woven label, milk caps/tassel/vintage

Ferne
Glass optometrist lens/Limited Edition Rubberstamps, Transparency sheet/Epson, Sheet adhesive/Therm O Web, Printed paper/Design Originals, Necklace pieced from vintage jewelry

Pages 50-51
Embellishing Photos
Roadside Attractions
Paper/Karen Foster Design, Background stamps/Hero Arts, Metallic blue ink/Clearsnap, Firework stamps/Clearsnap, Gold dust/Ranger, Alphabet stamps/Hero Arts, R stamp/Paper Candy, Embossing powder and glitter glue/Ranger, Tiny stars, eyes, metal buttons, Route 66 button/JHB International, Square brad/Creative Impressions, Blue nailheads/Karen Foster Design, Black metal dots/Limited Edition Rubberstamps, Tiny buttons/Karen Foster Design, Tiny gold marbles/Halcraft, Rhinestone/JewelCraft, Map, tickets, fake fur, guest check, bow tie, Statue of Liberty, stars, metal hat/vintage

Rose Lady Tin
Tin/found, Image/ARTchix Studio, Text/Collage Joy, Roses, beads/vintage, Glitter glue/Ranger

Party
Album/Canson, Printed paper/Collage Joy, Music paper/vintage, Tinsel/Magic Scraps, Press type/ChartPak, Metal letters/unknown, Corners/Creative Beginnings, Charms, sequins, ribbons/vintage

Pages 52-53
Photo Aging
Brian and Erikia
Printed paper/Design Originals, Stickers/Frances Meyer/Paper House Productions, Letter Stickers/Creative Imaginations, Glitter/Magic Scraps, Vintage photos/ARTchix Studio, Buttons, fabric appliqué, tape measure/vintage

"Happey" Home
Printed paper/Penny Black, Cork paper/Magic Scraps, Panoramic photographs/Creative Imaginations, Sunflower die cuts/Paper House, Productions, Stickers/Penny Black/Paper House Productions, Stamps/Inkadinkado/Hero Arts, Stamping ink/Ranger, Brass embellishments/Hot Off the Press, Rusted heart/USArtQuest, Key/vintage

Pages 54-55
Tearing and Reassembling Photos
Dream Car
Album/DMD, Papers/DMD/Emagination Crafts/Magenta/Paper Adventures, 4 Stamps/JudiKins, Ribbon-Scrappy's, Tags/American Tag/DMD, Letter R/Hot Off the Press, D &C stamps/Ma Vinci's Reliquary, M stamp/Queen of Tarts, Letter A sticker/Creative Imaginations, Charm/Boutique Trims. Fibers/DMC, Silver paint pen/Ranger, Wire, bottle caps and letter A/vintage

Be Happy Every Day
Album/Kolo, Mulberry papers and Printed vellum/NRN, Border stickers/Club Scrap/Magenta, Vellum envelopes/C-Thru Ruler, Butterflies/NRN, Silver accents/Hot Off The Press, Tag and Stamp/Limited Edition Rubberstamps, Real leaves/Nature's Pressed, Bee sticker/K and Company, Fibers/EK Success, "Be Happy Every Day" stamp/Hero Arts, Metal tin/found

Pages 56-57
Silhouetting Photos
Rockabilly Rebel
Embossed cardstock/DMD, Printed flame cardstock/NRN, Photo die cut/Paper House Productions, Car and guitar charm/Boutique Trims, Typewriter keys, vintage photo/ARTchix Studio, Alphabet, star nailheads/JewelCraft, Paper clip-/Cavallini and Co., Glitter glue/Ranger, Blue label/DYMO, Wood tag/American Tag Co., Slide mount/Loersch, Rebel pin/Button Pin, Photo paper/Epson, Sheet music/vintage

Tiny Treasures Box
Pill box/Apothecary Products Inc., Printed paper, epoxy stickers/Creative Imaginations, Mrs. Grossmans, Acrylic paint/Golden Artist colors, Photo paper/Epson, Checkered ribbon/Offray

Hilde
Bingo card/The Creative Block, Printed paper/Design Originals, Typewriter keys/ARTchix Studio, Decorative eyelets/Creative Imaginations, Beaded trim, rhinestones/JewelCraft, Scrabble word/Limited Edition Rubberstamps, Fibers/Rubba Dub Dub, Transparency paper/Epson

Ginseng Shrine Frame
Scrabble tiles, glass vials/Limited Editions, Rhinestones, jewelry findings/JewelCraft, Printed transparency/Magic Scraps, Printed vellum/NRN, Velvet paper/Paper Adventures, Metal wings/Boutique Trims, Wire/Artistic Wire, Foam adhesive/3L, Photo paper/Epson

Mom
Wearable scrapbook, letter stickers, watch sticker/Creative Imaginations, Script stamp/Hero Arts, Date stamp/Newell Office Supplies, Stamping inks/Clearsnap, Stamp punch/EK Success

Pages 58-59
Hand Coloring Photos
Butch 1948
Background page, wrapping paper, 3 Christmas images/found-vintage, Green mesh/Magenta, Green printed paper/Karen Foster Design, Background stamp, "Greetings" stamp and alphabet stamps/Paper Candy, Christmas seals/Queen of Tarts, Number stickers/Club Scrap, Fibers/EK Success, Ink/Clearsnap, Chalk/Craf-T

Samples
Colored pencils/EK Success, Markers/EK Success, Metallic Rub-ons/Craf-T, Glitter and gel pens/Sakura

Kitty Box
Frame box/All Night Media, Beads and rhinestones/JewelCraft, Colored collage pieces/Wonderland Emporium, Stamp/Magenta

Pages 62-63
Metal Stamping Letters
Love is a Game...
Cardstock/DMD, Printed paper/Magenta, Metal foil/AMACO, Steel letter stamps/Young Bros./Stamp Works Inc., Metallic Rub-ons/Craf-T, Adhesive/Glue Dots International, Eyelet tag Alphabet/Making Memories, Rubber stamps/Club Scrap/Stampers Anonymous, Stamping ink/Ranger, Mesh/Magic Scraps, Fiber/EK Success, Brads/Magic Scraps, Eyelets/JewelCraft, Playing cards/vintage

Time Flies
Printed papers, shaped metal tag rim/Creative Imaginations, Printed paper/Me and My Big Ideas, Metal foil/AMACO, Steel letter stamps/Harbor Freight, Metallic rub-ons/Craf-T, Adhesive/Glue Dots International, Watch face/ARTchix Studio, Wing charms/Boutique Trims, Binding discs/Rollabind, Stamping inks-Clearsnap

Laminate Samples, Decorating With…
Paper: Laminate chip/Therm O Web, Photographic die cut/Paper House Productions, Beads, sequins/JewelCraft, Wire/Artistic Wire, Words from book pages/vintage
Stickers: Laminate chip/Therm O Web, Stickers/Paper House Productions/Stampendous, Ribbon/Offray
Stamping: Laminate chip/Therm O Web, Stamp/All Night Media, Stamping ink, craft markers/Tsukineko, Rub-on brad decoration/Creative Imaginations
Embossing Powder: Laminate chip/Hardware store, Collage ephemera/FoofaLa, Scrabble tile word/Limited Edition Rubberstamps/UTEE, bitty beads/Ranger
Metal: Laminate chip/Hardware store, Transparency/ARTchix Studio, Label maker/DYMO, Decorative eyelet/Creative Imaginations, Charm/Boutique Trims, Tag/American Tag Co.

Pages 88-89
Paper Casting
Wild Child
Leopard print paper/unknown, Leopard print velvet paper/Grafix, Green and tan mulberry papers/Black Ink, Casting molds/Arnold Grummer, Leaf stamps/Hero Arts, Large and small alphabet stamps/Hero Arts, Paper butterflies/Wonderland Emporium, Ribbon/The Robin's Nest, Fibers/Rubba Dub Dub, Photo corners/Kolo, Chalks/Stampin' Up!, Dried flowers/Nature's Pressed, Dried leaves/All Night Media, Leaf buttons and butterfly charm/JHB International, Book page and leaf charms/vintage

Leaf and Dragonfly
Molds/Arnold Grummer

Pages 90-91
Adorning Paper Frames
Eldon
Printed paper/Club Scrap/Design Originals, Sticker quote/Club Scrap, Stamps, mini eyelets/Limited Edition Rubberstamps, Stamping ink/Tsukineko, Charms/Rubba Dub Dub/Boutique Trims, Nailheads/JewelCraft, Metal foil/AMACO, Steel letter stamps/Young Bros./Stamp Works Inc., Metallic rub-ons/Craf-T, Oval tag/C-Thru Ruler, Paper clips/Cavallini and Co, Foam adhesive/Stampin' Up!, Paper frame, key/vintage

Hunter
Printed paper/Reminiscence Paper, Crackel stamp/Stampin' Up!, Stamping ink/Tsukineko/Ranger, Punch/Emagination Crafts, Tag/American Tag Co., Tag, brad rub-ons/Creative Imaginations, Bone, letter charms/Boutique Trims, Steel letter stamps/Young Bros./Stamp Works Inc., Metallic rub-ons/Craf-T, Transparency/ARTchix Studio, Fiber/Making Memories, Office label maker/DYMO, Foam adhesive/3L, Paper frame/vintage

Brian and Erikia
Embossed paper/K & Company, Gel Medium/Golden Artist Colors, Paper frame, beads, buttons, typewriter font/vintage

Pages 92-93
Creating With Craft Plastic
Jeannie
Album/Canson, Craft plastic/Plaid enterprises, Pink and red papers/EK Success/Karen Foster Design/Paper Adventures/Reminiscence, Leopard print paper/Making Memories, Black/gold mesh paper/Magenta, Collage paper/DMD, Alphabet Stickers/Club Scrap, Number stamps/Hero Arts, Dymanicy label/Collage Joy, Quote sticker/Wordsworth, Leaf patterns stamp cube/Stampendous, Frame stamp/Magenta, Face stamps/Queen of Tarts, Pattern stamp/All Night Media, Flower punches/EK Success, Solvent ink/Tsukineko, Charms/ARTchix Studio/Boutique Trims, Glitter glue/Ranger, Slick writer marker/American Crafts, Checker pieces, feather, chopstick wrapper, woman/found/vintage

Las Vegas Picture Frame
Frame/Emagination Crafts, Red paper/Paper Adventures, Tiger stripes stamp/Rubber Stampede, Zig-zag pattern/unknown, Charms/Boutique Trims, Glitter glue/Ranger

Pages 94-95
Making Handmade Stamps
Cowboy Up
Book/vintage, Papers/Design Originals/Emagination Crafts/Karen Foster Design, Moldable foam/Penscore, Background stamp/River City Rubberworks, Corner stamp/Magenta, Alphabet stamps/Ma Vinci's Reliquary, Inks/Ranger, Large charms/Boutique Trims, Jute fibers/The Robin's Nest

Western Union
Card/DMD, Vintage Ephemera/Collage Joy/Queen of Tarts, Blank faux postage/Limited Edition Rubberstamps, Photo corners/Kolo, Censor stamp/River City Rubberworks, Cancellation stamp/River City Rubberworks, Charm/Limited Edition Rubberstamps, Ink/Ranger, Moldable stylus tip/Clearsnap

Pages 96-97
Mica Tile Transfers
Beadazzling
Printed paper, die cuts/NRN, Mesh paper/Magenta, Printed collage paper, quote/DMD, Gel medium, acrylic paints/Golden Artist Colors, Mica Tiles/USArtQuest,

Word, letter stickers/Stampendous, Copper tag/Limited Editions, Engraving tool for tag/Magic Scraps, Fibers/EK Success/Inkadinkado, Letter, number stamps/Hero Arts/Stamp Craft by Plaid, Stamping ink/Clearsnap, Colored Staples/Target, Charms/Boutique Trims, SX-70 film/Polaroid, Book, seam binding tape, images on mica/vintage

Art and Soul
Card, tag/DMD, Letter stamps/Ma Vinci's Reliquary/Limited Edition Rubberstamps, Stamping ink/Clearsnap, Printed vellum, paper, transparent stickers/NRN, Embossed paper/K and Company, Mica tile/USArtQuest, Gel medium/Golden Artist Colors, Ribbon/Offray

Pages 98-99
Embellishing With Clay
Floyd W. Miller
Printed paper/Club Scrap/Creative Imaginations, Handmade paper/Emagination Crafts, Polymer clay, templates/Polyform, Stamps/JudiKins, Stamping ink/Clearsnap, Photo die cut/Paper House Productions, Postage stamp stickers/Me and My Big Ideas, Fibers/Art Sanctum/EK Success, Charms/Boutique Trims, Nailheads/JewelCraft, Embossing foil/AMACO, Steel letter stamps/Harbor Freight, Metallic rub-ons/Craf-T, Canvas photo paper/Marshall's, Photo paper/Epson, Foam adhesive/3L

Gaiety Girl Journal
Album/DMD, Printed papers, epoxy sticker, border sticker, tag rub-ons/Creative Imaginations, Polymer clay/Polyform, Stamping inks/Clearsnap, Craft ink/Dr. Ph Martin's, Acrylic paint/Golden Artist Colors, Charms/ARTchix Studio, Ribbon/Offray, Torn fabric strips/vintage

Pages 100-101
Combining Elements
Lucky Cat
Papers/DMD, Vintage images/ARTchix Studio, Letter tiles/Hot Off The Press, Metal letters/Global Solutions, Background stamps/Raindrops On Roses, Paw stamp/unknown, Inks/Clearsnap, Metallic pen/Ranger, Black pen/Sakura

Copper Cat
Circle tag and arrow tag/DMD, Metallic rub-ons/Craf-T, Brass ovals/ARTchix Studio, Seed and bugle beads/JewelCraft, Black dots and square brad/Limited Edition Rubberstamps

Black Cat
Circle tag/DMD, Metallic rub-ons/Craf-T, Brown teardrops/Limited Edition Rubberstamps, Brass arrow and copper oval/ARTchix Studio, Copper eyelets/ScrapArts, Spiral nailheads/Jest Charming, Copper brad/Karen Foster Design, Charms/found

Gold Cat
Circle tag/DMD, Metallic rub-ons/Craf-T, Photo corners/Canson, Black square brad and tiny eyelets/Limited Edition Rubberstamps, Brass charm/ARTchix Studio

Floral Album Cover
Album/Kolo, Fibers/EK Success, Circle and washer/found, Beads/Rubba Dub Dub, Hearts and corners/Making Memories

Pages 102-103
Nature Printing
Enduring Friendship
Printed paper, mesh/Magenta, Printing ink/Ranger, Letter stamps/Inkadinkado, Stamping ink/Clearsnap, Paper clips/Cavallini and Co., Dictionary definition/Making Memories, White calligraphy ink/Dr. Ph. Martin's, Photo paper/Epson, Mini tag/DMD Industries, Dictionary pages, stamps/vintage

Sheri and Tasha
Printed paper/Reminiscence Papers, Printing ink/Ranger, Epoxy letter stickers, letter stickers/Creative Imaginations, Plastic discs/Rollabind, Nailheads/JewelCraft, Photo corners/Canson, Metallic Rub-Ons/Craf-T, Calligraphy ink-Dr. Ph. Martin's, Photo paper-Epson

Pages 104-105
Embossing Metal Mesh
Where Loveliness Is Found
Album/vintage magazine, Paper and stickers/Magenta, Metal mesh/AMACO, Background stamp/Clearsnap, Leaf and dragonfly stamps/Hero Arts, Nameplate stamp/Limited Edition Rubberstamps, Fig stamps/Ma Vinci's Reliquary, Ink and ultra-thick embossing powders/Ranger, Nailhead stickers/Stampendous

You Hold the Key
Album/Canson, Printed papers/Club Scrap/Paper Adventures, Mesh/AMACO, Hand Stamp/JudiKins, Writing stamp/Stampin' Up!, Key stamps/Limited Edition Rubberstamps/Wordsworth, Letter tiles/FoofaLa/Limited Edition Rubberstamps, Letter stamps/Queen of Tarts, Keys and hearts/found/vintage, Charms/Boutique Trims, Black dots/Limited Edition Rubberstamps, Ultra thick embossing powder/Ranger

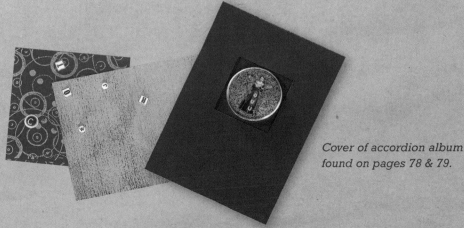

Cover of accordion album found on pages 78 & 79.

We would like to thank the following companies who made generous donations towards this book.

American Art Clay Co. (AMACO)
(800) 374-1600
www.amaco.com

American Tag Company
(800) 223-3956
www.americantag.net

Arnold Grummer
(800) 453-1485
www.arnoldgrummer.com

ARTchix Studio
(250) 370-9985
www.artchixstudio.com

Canson, Inc. (wholesale only)
(800) 628-9283
www.canson-us.com

Clearsnap, Inc. (wholesale only)
(360) 293-6634
www.clearsnap.com

Club Scrap, Inc.
(888) 634-9100
www.clubscrap.com

Collage Joy
collagejoy.com

Craf-T Products
(507) 235-3996
www.craf-tproducts.com

Creative Imaginations (wholesale only)
(800) 942-6487
www.cigift.com

C-Thru Ruler Co., The (wholesale only)
(800) 243-8419
www.cthruruler.com

Design Originals
(800) 877-0067
www.d-originals.com

DMD Industries, Inc. (wholesale only)
(800) 805-9890
www.dmdind.com

Dr. Ph. Martin's- a division of
Salis International, Inc.
(800) 843-8293
www.docmartins.com

EK Success™, Ltd.
(800) 524-1349
www.eksuccess.com

Emagination Crafts, Inc. (wholesale only)
(630) 833-9521
www.emaginationcrafts.com

Epson America, Inc.
www.epson.com

Fiskars, Inc. (wholesale only)
(800) 950-0203
www.fiskars.com

FoofaLa
(402) 758-0863
www.foofala.com

Glue Dots International (wholesale only)
(888) 688-7131
www.gluedots.com

Golden Artist Colors, Inc.
www.goldenacrylics.com

Hermafix distributed by J + V Enterprises
(801) 479-5939

Hero Arts® Rubber Stamps, Inc. (wholesale only)
(800) 822-4376
www.heroarts.com

Hot Off The press, Inc.
(800) 227-9595
www.craftpizazz.com

Hot Potatoes
(615) 269-8002
www.hotpotatoes.com

Inkadinakdo, Inc.
(800) 888-4652
www.inkadinkado.com

JewelCraft LLC
(201) 223-0804
www.jewelcraft.biz

JHB International, Inc.
(303) 751-8100
www.buttons.com

JudiKins, Inc.
(310) 515-1115
www.judikins.com

K & Company
(888) 244-2083
www.kandcompany.com

Karen Foster Design™ (wholesale only)
(801) 451-9779
www.scrapbookpaper.com

Kolo™, LLC
(888) 828-0367
www.kolo-usa.com

Limited Edition Rubberstamps
(650) 594-4242
www.limitededitionrs.com

Loersch Corporation
www.loersch.com

Ma Vinci's Reliquary
www.crafts.dm.net

Magenta Rubber Stamps (wholesale only)
(800) 565-5254
www.magentarubberstamps.com

Magic Scraps™
(972) 238-1838
www.magicscraps.com

Marshall's Arts & Crafts
(847) 821-0450
www.bkaphoto.com

NaturePrint Paper Products, Inc.
(925) 377-0755
www.natureprintpaper.com

NRN Designs
(800) 421-6958
www.nrndesigns.com

Paper Adventures® (wholesale only)
(800) 727-0699
www.paperadventures.com

Paper Candy
www.papercandy.com

Paper House Productions
(800) 255-7316
www.paperhouseproductions.com

Penny Black, Inc.
(510) 849-1883
www.pennyblackinc.com

Pioneer Photo Albums, Inc.®
(800) 366-3686
www.pioneerphotoalbums.com

Plaid Enterprises, Inc.
(800) 842-4197
www.plaidonline.com

Polyform Products Co.
(847) 427-0020
www.sculpey.com

Queen Of Tarts Stamps
www.queen-of-tarts.com

Ranger Industries, Inc.
(800) 244-2211
www.rangerink.com

Reminiscence Papers
(503) 26-9681
www.reminiscencepapers.com

River City Rubber Works
(877) 735-2276
www.rivercityrubberworks.com

Rollabind LLC
(800) 438-3542
www.rollabind.com

Rubba Dub Dub Artist's Stamps
(209) 763-2766
www.artsanctum.com

Sakura of America
(800) 776-6257
www.sakuraofamerica.com

Seasonal Expressions
A Boutique Trims Company
(888) 437-3888
www.BTCrafts.com

Stampendous!®/Mark Enterprises
(714) 688-0288
www.stampendous.com

Stampin' Up!®
(800) 782-6787
www.stampinup.com

Therm O Web, Inc.
(800) 323-0799
www.thermoweb.com

Toybox Rubber Stamps
(707) 431-1400
www.toyboxrubberstamps.com

Tsukineko, Inc.
(800) 769-6633
www.tsukineko.com

USArtQuest, Inc.
(517) 522-6225
www.usartquest.com

Wordsworth
(719) 282-3495
wordsworthstamps.com

Pamela Frye Hauer

Since childhood Pamela Frye Hauer has had a love for arts and crafts, especially those involving paper. She won her first art competition in the 3rd grade and has gone on to win many since. Beginning at the age of 15, she sold her artwork in local galleries. Following high school, she attended The Art Institute where she met her husband, as well as earned a degree in Graphic Design. After working in many creative fields, she began her professional relationship with Memory Makers in early 2000, creating artwork for their magazines, books, marketing department and television appearances. Pamela has also done freelance artwork for several product companies and recently consulted an international button distributor, designing and developing a line of their product marketed to scrapbookers. Pamela lives in Denver, Colorado with her husband Ronnie, son Milo and many pets in a 100-year-old house filled with collectibles.

Erikia Ghumm

Erikia's intense interest in arts and crafts of all kinds began in her childhood and followed her throughout her school years. While in high school, she married her longtime sweetheart and was inspired to create her first scrapbook documenting their love. After graduation she continued to pursue her art, showing her work in local galleries where it won numerous awards. In June of 1999, Erikia began working with Memory Makers. Since that time she has created hundreds of ideas, projects and pieces of artwork for the company's magazines, books, marketing department and television appearances. She currently enjoys working as a freelance scrapbook artist designing pages for numerous product companies and industry magazines, and teaching workshops at conventions around the country. Erikia lives with her husband of fourteen years, Brian; their dog, Hunter; and two cats, Sinatra and Baby, in Brighton, Colorado. She spends her spare time working in her home studio or collecting eclectic vintage items. She says her art continues to be inspired by her family and friends who have always played an important role in the direction of her work.

Index